D1211937

Forbidden Agendas

Forbidden Agendas presents a new approach to groupwork for consultants, therapists, psychodramatists, and teachers – anyone who works with groups. It is specially written for the person who is 'called in' when a group or organization is in trouble, or who is asked to run a group with special needs.

Antony Williams draws on his extensive experiences as a family therapist, teacher, and psychodramatist to provide safe action processes suitable for groups and organizations. He shows that the use of strategic action methods creates a space where spontaneity can thrive, and where group leaders can chip away at the 'forbidden agendas', the invisible loyalties that prevent group members from behaving constructively. Sometimes these loyalties have been formed long ago, pacts kept even with the dead; sometimes they are current, attempting to protect other people in the here-and-now of the group. The agendas operate blind, moles deep in the group unconscious, so that even those bound by them are 'forbidden' to be aware of their presence.

The book is designed to build on the leader's practical skills of 'warming up' a group for change, and is studded with examples, exercises, and alternative ways of encountering the challenges of change in groups. Full of practical suggestions, it will enable readers to 'find their voice' as group leaders: as the author writes, 'You find your voice, and the group does too.'

The author

A practising family therapist, teacher, and psychodramatist, Antony Williams is the author of *The Passionate Technique: Strategic Psychodrama with Individuals, Families, and Groups* (Routledge, 1989). He is a Senior Lecturer at La Trobe University, Melbourne, Australia.

Forbidden Agendas

Strategic action in groups

Antony Williams

TAVISTOCK/ROUTLEDGE
London and New York

First published 1991
by Routledge
11 New Fetter Lane, London EC4P 4EE

Simultaneously published in the USA and Canada
by Routledge
a division of Routledge, Chapman and Hall, Inc.
29 West 35th Street, New York, NY 10001

Typeset from author's disk by Columns of Reading
Printed and bound in Great Britain by
Mackays of Chatham PLC, Chatham, Kent

British Library Cataloguing in Publication Data

Williams, Antony, 1941–
Forbidden agendas : strategic action in groups.
1. Medicine. Drama therapy
I. Title
616.891523

Library of Congress Cataloging in Publication Data

Williams, Antony, 1941–
Forbidden agendas : strategic action in groups
by Antony Williams.
p. cm.
Includes bibliographical references.
1. Psychodrama. I. Title.
RC489.P7W53 1990
616.89′1523—dc20 90–8263
CIP

ISBN 0–415–04401–4
0–415–04402–2 pbk

To my students, my loves

Contents

Acknowledgements

Mary Good, Jude Murphy and Dan Rosenblatt kindly acted as critics when this book was first being formed. Gulping at the brickbats, and gratefully grasping the bouquets, I was confident that their old one-two treatment would work; I hope it has. Janie Forbes also screened parts of the manuscript, laughed at the jokes, patted my hand, and persuaded me that most of you would enjoy yourselves. I hope you do.

Many people conspired to help me, lending not just their hearts but their houses – Peter Dunn at Flinders; Mary Good in Melbourne; David Williams and Diana Spinks in Sydney; Dan Rosenblatt at Long Island, Maya Poirson in Paris, Joady Brennan and Peter Bartlett in Somerset, and Paddy Bade in London. And while it seems strange to thank an institution, which as such cannot read these words, I am grateful to La Trobe University for giving me opportunities to think and to write. It has also given me the opportunity, which I've taken, to become twenty-year cronies with Bernie, George, and Warren.

As this book is no accountant's ledger, it often fails specifically to record when I have tickled the till of others' works and when I have dreamed up something myself – the mines and the thines of two decades of learning and teaching have now passed into a fund marked 'current account' which I draw on every day. Even the 'original' contributions, though, are ultimately based on the cultures of strategic therapy and psychodrama, and I feel as proud of my debts to these two traditions as I do of attempting to create one myself. I trust I have distorted the ideas neither of Michael White, whose influence is pervasive, nor Gregory Bateson in my adaptations for groupwork. Max and Lynette Clayton's handwriting can be distinguished in the first chapter on warm-up, and theirs and George Calley's signature can also be detected in some of the sociometry exercises. The chapter on 'Strategic sociometry' is similar to an article I wrote for *Journal of Group Psychotherapy, Psychodrama and Sociometry*; my thanks to the editors for letting my reuse the material.

I have dedicated this book to my students, though sometimes 'my' seems an odd word to attach to 'students'. Like a family Christmas, our life together hasn't always been ideal; but more often than not our seminars had the air of children opening presents when they first wake up on that exciting December morning. Secretly, I have always felt that my pile under the tree was the biggest.

Introduction

If you start from a thought, that's the worst thing. Starting from a picture is better. Starting from a vague but exciting feeling is best of the lot. It'll get hold of you physically, it will dance you around.

Les Murray

Action

Though Les Murray was referring to writing poetry, he could have been revealing recipes for action methods: choosing a picture or a vague but exciting feeling from someone is 'best of the lot'. As the action takes over, and life slices to the preconscious bone, each of you grips on to your experience as best you can, and it will 'dance you around'. In a group run on action lines, members find a strange voice, which they begin to recognize as their own; they feel the gush of their life building up. . . . Is *this* who I am? They tell stories about themselves in terms of their personal or work-related problems. A revelation of the self to the self occurs as the group enacts its problem-sodden stories, maybe more fully than had ever seemed possible. The forbidden agendas, once inside and cloudy, are now outside, and clear. A new story is produced, and the two lie down, side by side.

Action will 'get hold of you physically', all right; and it will throw you on to others, too, instructing you once more in the mysteries of the human heart, and the patterns that connect human heart to human heart. In revealing the self to the self, culture is restored as well: the new stories almost always refer to different and healing links with others and contain the perennial springtime messages of how we are to be vital to, and with, each other. You see, the core of the dramatic method is irreducibly social; it creates as it goes a community to share in the performance of their lives. The acted story puts people in organic social contact, even when that contact is sometimes raw. Nevertheless, in all frailty and glory, members strive to be present to each other, finding heart in the heart of darkness. Life, maybe more than one would wish sometimes, fills the room, floods narrative, links one person to the other, and one story to the stories of humankind.

That little synopsis may sound rather obscure: the whys and hows of action consultation to groups are the focus of this book, which, like any story, will take some time to unfold. Some of the language – even words like 'story' itself – far less 'double description' or 'cybernetic' may seem strange, or are used in an unfamiliar way. In brief, this is a book about strategic consultancy to groups and organizations; the consultants use 'action methods' to help people replace their dysfunctional narratives or 'stories' with narratives that work better for them and the other people in their lives. A 'new story', of course, can be simply the old one, which once told fully, can be viewed afresh.

Social archaeology

Action methods take us to a site where we have never been, and stand us on the spot where a life happened – it sometimes seems more like archaeology than psychology. Whether the drama is contemporary – about one's organization, say – or historical, about one's family-of-origin, one has the sense of excavation of deep-buried personal societies. The warming-up process shows us shards, scrolls, and cooking utensils that seem as if they had been used only that very day. Director and protagonist enter an unknown milieu, and discover, little by little, its essence: persons are revealed in all their layers, not only of time but of character and relation to others. The archaeology is 'within' an individual person, too, as one sees this level laid over that, over that, over that. Why, it hardly seems at all like the person one met in the hall; was it only an hour ago?

Not even 'archaeology' is quite right. We are talking about action, here: the dust, the faint traces, and the digging itself feature only at the beginning. This shaft is one that is let down into real life. As we keep going through the layers, the family courtyard does not remain silent; one can smell the cooking, see people moving about, and hear the distant sounds of sex or an argument. All the rhythms and noises say that this is no dead civilization we are witnessing. People new to action groups are often stunned by the power of the process, the depth of feeling, the beauty of the tableaux, the 'reality' of its sparse scenery (tables and chairs, usually), and the way a drama reaches far into the heart of a person's history. Through that person's, it gets to all our histories.

Genuine dramas cannot but arouse feelings of pity, admiration, and awe at the human story. Their systemic base makes them true psychological 'who-dunnits' rather than the 'why-dunnits' of some types of individual psychology. The rich sedimentary layerings of one person's history on another's, when revealed by the dramatic method cause not just the protagonist, but the audience too, to feel a profound emotional rapport with what is going on. Culture is being restored to itself. Fake, sentimental, or ugly dramas do just the opposite, of course.

Thought into action – externalization/concretization

Copying of experience is not the point – the acting of narrative and stories is not so much mimetic as *transformational* (Schechner, 1988); what cannot take place anywhere else is created or incarnated in a special place – the group. Action in groups does not so much 'depict' as suggest and interpret the world, just as a painting does (except we are used to that idea in a painting, whereas psychological workers sometimes give themselves much credit for 'uncovering' reality in therapy or consultancy). To some extent, then, the archaeological 'dig' is an archaeological 'plant'; it is not a mirror of life, but a new version of life. The concrete representation of narrative becomes the basis of aesthetics, sociometry, and the warming-up process (group 'warm-up' is a way of getting the group's heart to beat in time with its concerns, and sociometry is a way of assessing and influencing what is going on in the group – large sections will later be devoted to each of these as topics in their own right).

What a nice little kid

M: *When I was five I saw my dog get run over. I caused it by calling him at the wrong time. All I could see was this fur flying up in the air. . . . I'll be doing something, and then all of a sudden a big bit of memory will hit me. . . . The only bits I can remember are awful bits. I have photos of myself as a kid. I look at them and I smile but I cry at the same time. I think: O Jesus, what a nice little kid she was after all (cries).*

D: *Choose someone to be that dog. (M does so.)*
Can you describe for me where all this took place. Set up the scene just as you remember it, using chairs and tables – whatever's here – to represent the things that were there (she does this, taking her time). Now, let's have that little kid out here. . . .

The type of interaction between the director and member may be familiar to you: M has begun a narrative and D starts to build an action sequence from its simplest base – 'concretization' or 'externalization'. In action, there is always a self and an object outside the self, whether that be a person, Spirit, quality, or another 'part' of the speaker. A meeting takes place where the other (for example, that 'little kid') is 'externalized' and given living form by the director, so that dialogue can begin.

Is this 'psychodrama', then? Not necessarily. The distinctions between psychodrama and 'action methods' are sometimes rather fine. Indeed some authors (e.g. Neville, 1989) maintain that all acting on behalf of the psyche is psychodrama, and others take action methods as the umbrella term, and psychodrama as a particular instance. There is no great scientific debate on the matter, however, so I will say how I am using the term in this book: any procedures involving externalization will be referred to as 'action methods'. Action methods characteristically dramatize narrative by means of dialogue and role reversal; events, problems, other people, or parts of the self are represented concretely (externalized), and an action in space and time is initiated.

In action methods, as distinct from psychodrama, the action may only last a short time, and does not usually involve the introduction of family-of-origin. It may be group-centred rather than individual-centred, and could even be a simple illustration of a point – explaining or teaching something, perhaps, by having chairs or cushions representing two sides of a debate or two scientific theories. Mostly, there tends to be a bit of moving around, and the taking up of roles. The versatility and colour of action make contrasts clearer, allow new points of view to emerge, and can inject an exhilarating air of experimentation and play. At the same time, their ability to be safe and low-key makes action methods suitable for groups, organizations, or classrooms where there is no commitment to psychodrama as such, and where indeed the processes of a full psychodrama would be inappropriate.

Concretization is an incarnation: the words become flesh and are taken on by an auxiliary. When a problem, a metaphor, or an object is 'outside', a dialectic is automatically created which eventually leads to a 'double description'. Double description is one of the bases of change in cybernetic theory and will be progressively described throughout the book. Its beginnings, though, can be illustrated now: the director, Dot, is talking to a member, Mitch, who seems withdrawn and troubled.

Scared poking

D: *Before we start, let's just get a bit clearer on what you are looking at.*

M: *I don't know. It's just me, I suppose.*

D: *Choose someone in the group to be 'just you'. (He does so; chooses Al.) Now choose someone to be the group.*

M: *That's hard. . . . Marnie, I think.*

D: *Fine. Now, is the group standing or sitting?*

M: *Mmmm, er. . . .*

D: *Reverse roles, be the group, and show what you are doing.*

M: *(As group, sarcastically) In this group we're going to be really nice, no matter what. There won't be any contentious issues.*

D: *Reverse roles and be yourself again. . . . Now, where do you put yourself in relation to the group?*

M: *Sort of, at the moment, poking.*

D: *Poking?*

M: *Scared poking.*

D: *Say that to the group.*
M: *I'm not sure whether I'm ugly to you. But I'm losing patience with the way you are.*
M: *(As group, in an exaggeratedly placating tone) Oh no, you're fine. Let's talk about something else.*

Reader, what do you make of it? Dissociated? Brilliant? Soppy? Firm? An example such as this triggers so many associations, questions, and judgements in us all. What Mitch and Dot did, even in such a brief interaction, is likely to draw you in to your own warm-ups as human beings and as experts in leading groups. Dot splits Mitch into two beings ('Choose someone in the group to be "just you"'), and then goes to his immediate interpersonal context – the group, thus instituting the potential for multiple descriptions and for action. She has externalized the complaint of 'just me, I suppose', and has produced at least one likely interlocutor, the group. Mitch quickly warms up to his deep fear ('I'm not sure whether I'm ugly to you'), and anger at himself and the group ('there won't be any contentious issues' . . .'I'm losing patience with the way you are'). Dot and Mitch have rapidly expanded the 'just me' into drama and dialogue.

Is any of this worthwhile? After all, group leaders working in any therapeutic modality are not exempt from human folly, greed, or stupidity. The methods they choose can be as shallow and naive as any other nostrum, promising a rose garden and delivering a cesspool. Group warm-ups and enactments, too, are sometimes irrelevantly narcissistic (see 'Warm-up to what?'), canonizing the very problems they attempt to solve. But at least when it is the 'real thing' out there, and it often is, witnessing narratives of the human condition is an elevating experience. Somehow, genuine narratives tow behind them in a cart called 'Drama', all the gravity and truth-to-experience of life itself. It is almost impossible to harden your heart against a 'true' drama, because they are the archetypal stories of our own love, struggle, and suffering being told. On the level of sharing what it is to be a human being, then, any honest drama is worthwhile for itself, just as a good poem, play, opera, or novel is.

What sort of book is this?

This is a book that attempts to help you with technique, so that when technique is fully accessible, you can 'find your voice' as a group leader (see Chapter 7). To reach the freedom of your own voice as a group consultant, you need technique and experience. Only when you know what you are doing, in blood and in brain, can you echo Gerard Manley Hopkins' 'What I do is me, for that I came'. It is said that Chinese scribes used to write with a chrysanthemum before them on their desks, so that their work might absorb some of the flower's own beauty, softness, and strength. This book aims to develop the beauty, softness, and strength of your group technique so that your voice can be helpful to others. (Some might consider it a real plus for chrysanthemums that once you get them going, they grow like weeds. Even more to the point: they last for ages, just as the effects of successful consultancy last.)

Firstly, beauty: the final chapter will be explicitly devoted to the aesthetics of change (not that it becomes less of a mystery as a result). Because the method is so visual and physical, beauty becomes paramount, even when it is of the stern and terrrible variety – a successful consultancy, like a life, is a dance of interacting parts, and requires form, poetic logic, and unity. Losing sight of the aesthetics almost certainly means weakening the consultancy. By 'aesthetics' I do not mean 'making it pretty', or adding bravura touches here and there. In fact, making one's work too fancy usually means interfering with the delicacy and force that is implicitly present in the story. Beauty is not merely softness and lyricism, but structure and strength, too.

The chrysanthemum image also suggests that your work can glow and be serious at the same time. As the change resulting from a consultancy needs to be durable, making groupwork pragmatic is as important as making it beautiful (they are not necessarily separate, anyway). So this is a kitchen sink of a book, designed to build on your practical skills – how to manage double description, externalization, warm-up, action, and sociometry. Most of the chapters are studded with examples, exercises, and alternative ways of encountering the challenges of pragmatic change in groups. You can use it as an explaining type of book, or a teaching and practice type of book.

The focus is working in groups, rather than the development of particular psychodramatic skills. Action methods are not psychodrama, and in this book only one full psychodrama (that of Maja, in Chapter 1) is reported. You may find even that drama 'linear' and apparently lacking in voluptuousness – it is used to explain some of the principles of change that will later be applied to groupwork proper, and is not representative of the full variety of the method. If you are seeking literature on psychodrama as such, you will not find much of it here. The original psychodrama literature can be found in Moreno's *Psychodrama, Vols I, II and III* (J. L. Moreno was the founder of psychodrama, bringing the method from Europe to the United States in the twenties). You can find more detailed accounts of how psychodrama works in *The Passionate Technique* (Williams, 1989a), and in other sources such as Blatner (1989) or Starr (1977), to name but three. Jonathan Fox (1987) has edited a first-class set of readings by Moreno, and Rene Marineau (1989) has produced a revealing and not always edifying biography of the man.

Although the entire book is about groupwork, I have divided it into two sections: in the early part you will see some cybernetic ways of focusing on and assisting individuals in a group, and in the second section you can learn and practise methods of consulting to the group as a whole. The more novel theoretical material is contained in the first part, and traditional practices (warm-up, sociometry, etc.) are examined in the second. All in all, the rationale for groupwork based on concretization, story, and double description may seem very strange to you at first, and so I have reversed the usual order of things. Remote preparation for the group, the tasks of the leader, the leader's own warm-up, and procedures to get a group going are all described in Part II, so that they might be understood in the light of the theory given in the first part. If these are your most direct interests, however, you could hightail it to Chapter 6 and read the text as a treatment of conventional group action skills.

Strategic action consultancy

In the strategic approach the consultant designs a particular set of tactics for each problem. The consultancy is based on an analysis of the nature of the problem, and the clients' unique constructs and solution patterns. The work is often contrary to conventional wisdom – especially conventional therapeutic wisdom. Strategic consultants take responsibility for directly influencing their clients, although, as you will see from the next chapter on, the client also retains a firm hand on the tiller whether the consultant likes it or not.

In the strategic mode, directors attempt to present each member with a set of circumstances within which spontaneity is most likely to take place. They chip away at the forbidden agendas, the invisible loyalties, that seem to compel clients to behave in ways that make them unhappy. Sometimes the invisible loyalties are to other people in the group, and sometimes they are back home (or even back in the family-of-origin home). As I remarked in *The Passionate Technique*, strategic workers tend to hold interactional and circular views of causality that free them from having to blame anybody – not the group member, and not the group member's mother either.

You may wonder why I do not just call you a 'group leader', and have done with it. As will be elaborated in Chapter 4, this is because of strategic workers' concern that there should be a specific problem to work on, whose resolution would mean the end of the work or the need for a new contract. 'Group leader' has more the feel of permanence to it, and throughout the book you will become aware of strategic fears of canonizing problems by yet more therapy. There is no harm in working long, if that is what the problem takes; but there is no great virtue in 'secondary victimization' of clients by never-ending treatment, where all they learn is that they need more consultancy or treatment.

So I am imagining, Reader, that you are the sort of person asked to lead groups or to act as consultant to organizations. I have settled for calling you a 'director' or a 'consultant', picturing you as working short-term in a group, or working in a short-term group. That is, the book is especially designed for a person who is 'called in' when a group or organization is in trouble, or who is asked to run a group with special needs, say, from one to six sessions – a morning to a weekend. Longer-term groups that are set up for supervision or teaching (for example, training groups which of their nature take place over a fixed time) provide exceptions to this short-term focus: these types of groups fit because they do in fact have a 'problem' orientation – how to learn something – and ways of knowing when you have 'got there'.

You will encounter plenty of examples and training exercises (you may want to skip these latter if you are not training) so that you will be able to build your sense of the method from its very basics – concretization, interaction, space, time, and movement. Sometimes, the examples come first and the explanation later. This is but to follow the method, which starts with action and leads to full involvement . . . *then* you make sense of what is happening or has happened.

It may be clear to you already that groups running on action have different features from those based purely on conversation. They recognizably belong to the same family, but are far from identical twins. Despite the differences between action groups and conventional groups, however, not much has been published on the action phases of groupwork – unless you count books of potted warm-up exercises. So if you are a first-time traveller in groupwork, you may need a caveat before you read further: you cannot rely on finding all you need to know about groupwork in this place. This is partly because others – notably Yalom (1975), Agazarian and Peters (1981), and Whitaker (1985) have already managed these themes quite splendidly. Adding to the already huge literature on long-term conversation-based groupwork, by me at least, would not be helpful. Nevertheless, 'group dynamics' are the fat pastures for forbidden agendas and usually the reason that the consultant is called in in the first place. How to assess and where need be alter dysfunctional dynamics is addressed pervasively in the book, and more specifically in 'Failure in warm-up' and in the four chapters on sociometry.

Storying and re-storying

The third basis for this book is the notion that persons give meaning to their experience by means of 'story'. If people are not to be overwhelmed by bombarding experience, they have to make sense by cutting most of it out, and pasting the rest into familiar shapes. Otherwise they would 'blank out' within a few seconds from sensory overload. All of us make sense even of apparently simple objects like this – by censorship and appliqué we get a 'story': we say 'my favourite chair', and 'that reliable old clock on the mantel', and 'my husband', and hope we do not get them mixed up. We do the same with events, relationships, and even that primary object – us.

Experience is not even experience until it is experienced – that is, 'storied' in some way. The process is not entirely promiscuous: we begin to take on dominant narratives that we tell ourselves; others tell back to us similar narratives, and thus we form what is known as 'culture' – whether it be of a national identity, a family, a group, or an organization. Some of these stories allow us to expand; others, alas, shrink us. For example, 'I am a no-good worthless person', or 'Our family is very close and strangers are a danger to it', or 'I can never love a man because my father was evil' are descriptions that cut off certain other descriptions. They cause us to blanket parts of our lived experience as 'not storyable', and to select only certain events as belonging to 'our story'. A compliment, a teenager wanting to branch out, or affectionate feelings towards a man cannot even be heard, acknowledged, or felt.

I was recently drinking tea on a verandah on a hot day, and talking to an old friend, Francine, who works in theatre but has a strong interest in matters therapeutic. Believe it or not, we were discussing the nature of information, change, and the unconscious. 'Is this what you mean?' she asked, and told me a story. Francine could not be described as shy: 'Put it in your book, if you like,' she said. So here it is:

The woman who stank

Francine, a single woman in her forties, is heading for a luncheon date with a very important new lover, Lance. As she drives, she begins to feel utterly unlovable, to the extent that she physically stinks to herself. Her clothes smell, her breath smells, her crotch smells, her armpits smell, her feet smell, her hair smells, even her teeth smell. She knows that she is quite unsuited for company of any sort, far less that of glamorous Lance.

Fortunately, her Guardian Angel pops the idea in her mind that at least some people do like her. This information is allowed 'in', and she relaxes a little. Almost immediately another thought enters: 'Oh, oh, this is how my mother always *felt'. It dawns on her at that moment that her mother believed that as a child she had killed her brother (who had died when he was 7 and she was 5). The stench lifts and leaves through the car windows. Francine feels her vitality return, and she begins to look forward to the date.*

Are Francine's changes an example of storying and re-storying? Only partly. True, she had many different ideas and underwent several emotional shifts in a short time: the fantasy that she smelt, and the questioning as to why this was so; the memory of loving friends, and the relaxation that followed that; the connection with her mother and dead uncle (which is as obscure to me, Reader, as it probably is to you; nevertheless, Francine is, how should one put it? – a temperamental person, and it does not do to question her too closely as a friend). Though these were all changes brought about by 'information', I am concerned with structures whereby change is usually more than the rapid play of thought upon thought that Francine experienced. My concern is with an 'outsider' changing fixed problematic behaviour, and getting those changes to stay around. It would be nearer the mark if one supposed that Francine was a person attending a group for those who were incapacitated in social interaction because of some debilitating notion about themselves. In Francine's case, say, it was that she *always* thought that she smelt when she was about to meet someone: imagine that through action methods she was able to discover different ways of dealing with her anxiety, or even to leave her anxiety behind on the hallstand or pinned on her mother's cardigan when she went on a date.

I will argue (taking a line from family therapist Michael White and ultimately from anthropologist Gregory Bateson) that any change in living systems comes about as a result of information. That sounds pretty simple: you just talk more, eh? . . . tell 'em how you feel. But the practice of getting information (a new story) to other people is not as easy as the encounter/dialogue psychologies of the sixties and seventies would have it. Any parent trying to correct a teenager's habits (to untidy son: 'How many times do I have to tell you to clean up your room!'; or, more seriously, to anorexic daughter: 'Eat, dear. If you don't eat, you'll have to go back to hospital and be put on a drip again.') will readily let you know the flaws in such a theory. Even though the parents (and I) would readily validate the importance of knowing what one is feeling, and having the courage to communicate it when appropriate, communication of how their behaviour is affecting you, and listening as deeply as one can to them, seems to make little difference: the son does not tidy the room and the daughter does not eat. The story they are telling themselves excludes yours, somehow.

How is this? I will be saying that we select from a limited range of our lived experience for our stories. We are restrained or 'forbidden' from seeing the world in ways other than the ways in which we now see it, usually because of our alliances with someone else and their stories. These alliances may have been formed long ago, and can even be answering cries from the past, pacts kept with people who are now dead. The forbidden agendas may also be protecting, helping, or obeying other people in the here-and-now, though this 'assistance' is most usually out of conscious awareness. You see, access to the forbidden agendas may be forbidden even to us who operate on them. They are moles deep in our personal constructs.

This book puts the notion of storying and re-storying side by side with action methods. It starts with an unusual drama about a woman called Maja – the only complete drama reported – and then goes back to the basics of action methods, taking in the topics of externalization, social atom, warm-up, failure in warm-up, classical sociometry, strategic sociometry, and supervision. I try to link these group processes with the notions of restraints, information, news of difference, and forbidden agendas.

Reader, I cannot do much about helping you find your own voice in all this. Maybe it is like poetry: remember how Les Murray suggested that you start from 'a vague but exciting feeling'. Robert Frost called it 'a lump in the throat, a homesickness, a lovesickness'. I cannot help you find that lump, the lovesickness. But perhaps I can help you with technique: the lump, the lovesickness can take the protective colouring of form as you help the protagonist get together the words and actions of the story. To paraphrase Seamus Heaney, your work is marked, is 'watermarked' with you: your essential perception, your stance on life, your feeling, memory, and experience. You find your voice, and the group does too. You search out that old story, and tell it to each other and the group. And then you and I may be able to agree on ways wherein a second story, perhaps more useful than the first, can become 'information', which allows people to change their lives for the better.

Part one

The act of change

Chapter one

Experiencing thinking

The iron chain and the silken cord are both equally bonds.

Schiller

Reader, if you, like me, are the sort of person who never reads introductions, you will not know that the first part of this book focuses on action work with 'individuals' in a group, and the second is concerned with consultation to the group as a whole. In this first part you will find more 'theoretical' explanation than in the second, but explanation may not be such a dire necessity as to prevent you flipping straight to Chapter 6 and reading about warm-ups and sociometry. I will be unpacking various wares from the cybernetic suitcase for five chapters, but if you did not want to look, nothing dreadful would happen to you, just as no harm befell you for not reading the Introduction. You could skip the whole book . . . you could skip every other book, too, and just take your own bible, whatever it is, wherever it is you are going.

Perhaps there is less choice in this than one imagines. The theme of this chapter and indeed of the whole work is the construction of truth – how we select and edit the stories that become the books of our 'bible'. Do not let this book become your bible, for there is not a word of truth in it – there is no word of 'truth' in your bible, either, if it comes to that.

This first chapter observes the interaction of a woman called 'Maja' with a director called 'Don'. Their narrative is used as a packhorse to carry some of the tools of working strategically; these tools will later be used on other sites, and finally on that intricate buried city of group-as-a-whole. But start with an easier dig – a story of two stories. The commentary focuses on the first story that Maja tells herself as she becomes warmed up to her relationship with her mother and the second story that she and Don co-create. Although much of the drama is spent in fashioning Maja's story about her 'past', Don is interested in what story Maja will tell herself in the future. The general relevance of 'story' and 'information' to group consultancy is developed more fully in Chapter 2. As for our pair – you will see in a few moments that Don is keen to build the second story out of the 'exceptions' of the first. Maja tells him when a painful experience *does* happen; he is curious to know when it does not. They struggle over the site of the dig, but begin to agree what new building could be erected there.

Maja's secret

In the second day of a professional two-day group on action methods in family therapy, one of the members, Maja, looks agitated. The theme for the day had been loss of significant others, and 'holes' in the social atom. Another group member, Mandy, had shortly before enacted a drama which revolved around missing her friends in another country: back home after a two-year study visit to the United States, Mandy had been overwhelmed by the hardship of getting a new set of friends together who would be as lively and as loving as her previous set. Mandy's drama had ended by her bidding emotional farewells to her friends and mentor.

After the 'sharing phase' (see The Passionate Technique *for a fuller description of this process) following Mandy's drama, the group had begun to discuss loss in the family, including the losses between parent and child that come about at each stage in a child's development.*

During this discussion, Don spots Maja looking pained and preoccupied. When he asks what is 'going on' for her, Maja replies that she is 'moving in and out' of raising an issue about her mother. Don asks her to show this on stage.

Don's invitation to 'show this on stage' does not necessarily mean that a full-length drama will follow; to enact a metaphor is a way of working in itself, based on a philosophy that Maja will get somewhere if action, however minimal and brief, is used. She will connect different contexts of experience, which will lead her to the sort of 'surprises' that enhance opportunities for spontaneity. Don is not trying to go beyond Maja's language, but to stay with it, to backlight strands in her web of symbolic meanings. By taking her language seriously, by entering it, Don and Maja find that it becomes not less mysterious, but more. And by embedding her language within the dramatic mode, Maja's predictable universe becomes suddenly unknown, demanding experiment and a radical approach.

Once on stage, Maja stands a few feet away from her mother. She goes forward a couple of steps, and then returns to where she had started. She repeats this several times, getting the feel of it.

She tells Don that her mother is out visiting her from Europe. It is her first visit since Maja herself emigrated eight years before. It is also probably her last, since her mother is old and frail, and would probably not be able to make the journey again. For political reasons, neither Maja, her husband, or her daughter have been back to their homeland since emigrating.

We can note already the thematic continuity (loss of relationship and loss of country) between Maja's warm-up and Mandy's drama of a few hours before. To this, Maja adds a new element of *ambivalence in relationship*.

M: I want to get near, but when I do, she binds me, and I have to move back.
D: Have you ever worked in a drama on your mother before?

You would expect Don to pick up on this 'binding' metaphor. It may therefore surprise you that at this stage he carefully avoids it, though he notes the phrase. He believes that to launch straight into that theme, albeit such an important one in psychology, might deflect him from the frame (of noting 'exceptions' to the first story) that he is already deciding will be most helpful.

Reader, you are more in a box seat than he, and you will be able to observe the perseverance of the metaphor of 'binding', and how it will keep knocking until the door is opened. Poor Don is at ground level, half blinded by a process that he has already decided upon. You see, although Don works with metaphor, he cannot, and does not have to, follow every metaphor that Maja throws out – simply to expand Maja's language system is not his aim. Like yourself, he is guided by constructs that will cause him to focus on particular parts of the story and to ignore others. Don's process, however, may be a little unfamiliar to you: he is interested in Maja's 'attempted solutions' (what she has tried to do to get over her problem), which he now knows have included the solution of at least one previous consultancy on the matter. He wants to find whether the previous solutions have been successful or not.

If there has been no change at all, then Don would have to consider whether it was worthwhile to proceed further: to go on in the face of previous no-change might be to set himself up as succeeding where others had failed. Such a position is a dangerous one, not so much because of Don's ego or even of 'wasting group time', but because as a group they might go through a process of entrenching a restrictive solution, and then 'canonizing' it in the session. The concepts of enabling and restrictive solutions will be elaborated more fully later.

By 'canonizing' something, I mean giving it an official seal of approval, in the way that, when the Catholic Church canonizes a person as a saint, it says that this person really was holy, really did do miracles, and really did choose the right solutions. A restrictive solution canonized by Holy Mother Therapy becomes set in stone: 'My therapist says that I am having the difficulties I'm having because of my early relationships with my dad.' Therapy is probably better preoccupied with spontaneity than with setting things, including explanations, in stone. Don is trying to avoid being Holy Mother anything. As you will see, in fact Maja *did* change as a result of her previous consultancy, and so Don has found the 'exception' to the complaint:

M: *Most of my dramas have been about my relationship with my father, and about his cruelty to me. I have done a little on my mother, chiefly about her not protecting me from my father.*

D: *What was the result of your work on your mother in your last drama? What changed after that?*

Don senses, though regrettably does not ask, that Maja may be seeking 'redressive action' (Turner, 1974) – a replication and critique of events leading up to a crisis, followed by a 'squaring of the books' through performance of public ritual payback. Retribution and transgenerational debt (Boszormenyi-Nagy and Spark, 1973) are themes of many psychodramas, and I have attempted to identify their usefulness as therapy in *The Passionate Technique*, pp. 117–118. In brief, the aim of redressive dramas is ultimately to reintegrate the person back to their social atom once the negative transgenerational debts have been settled. This ambition is fine, but, like anything else, can be an oft-resorted-to solution that becomes a problem in itself. Don has other fish to fry.

It seems that when she had first emigrated, Maja had written only to her father, who was the person in the family given the role of writing and receiving letters, even though Maja's relationship with him had been strained. When her father died, Maja had for a long time been unable to write to her mother. For months she had sat in front of her blank airletter pad. Then, as a result of her most recent drama, several years before, she finally did write. Mother and daughter at last began to correspond. She reported these letters as being 'unsatisfactory', and the communication 'thin' between them.

Don uses Maja's replies to the question 'Have you ever worked in a drama on your mother before?' in a way that will actually determine the type of story he will co-create in the next few minutes: Maja's answers give him a lead as to how to work strategically. Don's own map of what is 'helpful' not only influences what he says to Maja, but what Maja says to him. Consultants define and even create many of the quandaries dealt with in consultancy. Don's very decision to select Maja from the group because in some way she appeared to him to be 'warmed up' is probably based on many factors: on a non-conscious link between him and her; on her presuppositions of what a group was all about; on his presuppositions on the same subject, and indeed on the expectations and assumptions of the group itself. Somehow, in the six hours or so that they have been together, this edifice of meaning and expectation has all been created. It is, even in that short time, so shared a reality that no one questions it. The group has formed a *culture*, which can be for good or ill.

What Don asks about, ignores, and decides to dramatize affects the shape of the drama quite as much as Maja's narrative in itself. Indeed, as you have doubtless already observed, even her own narrative would *have* to have been different had Don asked her different questions. Were he a conventional psychodramatist, for example, he may have immediately suggested that she set up a scene of painful communication between her and her mother, and develop that scene as fully as possible, with all its anger and disappointment. If the group had been a 'talking therapy' group, of course, there would have been no scene or action at all, but other group members may have chimed in about their relationships with *their* mothers, and Don may have made some interpretations. If the group had been based on 'encounter', Don may have challenged Maja on what her dealings with her mother had 'to do with us, here and now'. If he had been running the group according to Bion's (1961) principles, he may have construed Maja's actions, or indeed his own, as 'flight'.

The list of 'ifs' could go on indefinitely. Clearly any one of these actions on Don's part would affect not only the definition of the problem and its perceived causes, but also the likely solutions that the group would take up: act the problem out; understand its meaning in the group-as-a-whole; encounter others in the here-and-now, and so on. So it is not just Maja who 'discovers' the problem; the group and Don have a hand in it too, even though Maja's 'problem' takes place outside the group, and presumably pre-existed it. It may already be clear to you that 'discoveries' in a group are also creations. One does not merely *find* treasure (or trash) in one's stories; one makes it on the spot, and over and over again.

D: Did anything change?
M: I began to write a little more about myself.
D: And what happened to your mother's replies?
M: No . . . yes. She began to say more about herself. It was not very much, and I would like more. She never would talk to me (she begins to reminisce about the deficiencies in her mother's communication with her).
D: (Interrupting) When did this change take place?
M: What change?
D: The change in her letter-writing to you.
M: About a year ago, I suppose, and now of course she's out visiting us.

So far we have concentrated mostly on Don. But naturally Maja, too, has played her part in creating not only the 'distance' between her and her mum, but also in construing that this was a problem at all. This view may sound shocking – after all, how can a mother and daughter's distance and difficulty in communication not be a problem? Certainly, Maja's talk to herself says that it should be otherwise, and many of us would have similar beliefs. But she could tell herself a different story – for example, that although her relationship leaves a lot to be desired, it is better than before; or that she may expect too much of her mother, or that the distance is from her own side, or that it suits her quite well to be relatively distant, or that if they get close they get too entangled in each others' psyches, and so on. Many different stories are possible, apart from the one which says it is necessary to tackle this problem head-on.

The description or 'story' about the relationship that Maja tells herself determines the relationship. It might be said that Maja's narrative of the relationship, rather than the relationship itself, is what is causing her the problem. This does not mean that she is not unhappy, or that things could not be better between the two, or, heaven forbid, that she is insincere. But she, like all of us, is managed by her beliefs and cannot attend to the exceptions to her problem-saturated (White, 1988) description of her relationship with her mother. At the moment she is not free to believe anything else; she is 'restrained' from telling herself a different story, and these restraints act as a break on her spontaneity. There are forbidden agendas that prevent her from seeing or enacting a different reality. Inadvertently, and with the best will in the world, she participates in the survival of the problem.

On a more concrete level, her explanation to herself that things are bad with her mother has not allowed her to realize that the relationship has actually changed. She is somehow unable to notice these things – the increased letter writing, the different content of the letters, the visit itself – because her *restraints*, most of them outside her consciousness, will not allow her to do so. Don is working away at these restraints, seeing if he can introduce any elasticity, so that Maja can pick out other descriptions or stories that will lead her to be happier.

Don's principal elasticizer is called 'double description' (White, 1986). He wants to get some distinction between what 'is' happening and Maja's interpretations of what is happening. He chooses as his point of entry the dialectic between what has happened recently and what has happened in the more distant past. Of course, even the word 'happened' should have inverted commas around it, since events cannot be distinguished from descriptions of events. There are many experiences – events, feelings, ideas, intentions, and so on that somehow have not been selected for survival (Bateson, 1979). What *has* survived is only one description or story. According to Don's notion of consultation, people can only change when they perceive a difference between something and something else. Don tries to bring a contrast between one story that Maja tells, and another, created on stage, so that she can forge descriptions that are not as oppressive as her current ones.

Don's enquiries have given a lead. He does not want the drama to end with Maja learning more dysfunctional roles than those with which she started, even though Maja herself is half asking for canonization of her woes. Reader, you will be shocked at how often this happens in groups: people, though sometimes in great pain, seem only to want confirmation of the impossibility of their situations. We grow fond of our stories, no matter how miserable – at least it is *our* misery, and therefore familiar. This is fairly conventional wisdom – we could hear it over the back fence. But the truth is that some protagonists are used to despair and not getting anywhere; they may even find difficulty recognizing the place if they did get somewhere. This is not because of ill will or bad moral character, but because the first story's power includes the epilogue that there can be no story but this one. That is not such a conventional view, because it includes the notion of restraints.

A consultant's preliminary and utterly important task, as you will see in the next chapter, is at least to acknowledge fully the first story – otherwise the system will eject the 'outsider' (the director) as not part of it, and therefore not having any information that will be in its interests to absorb. But it is equally important that the second description recognizes the changes in the desired direction that *have* occurred. Otherwise, there is some danger that these changes will be wiped out by the consultation itself. It becomes one more failed attempted solution, but a particularly dangerous one because of its power to canonize problems.

You see, Don is working on the pattern of the story that Maja tells herself, and then on the *exceptions* to the pattern (Lipchik and de Shazer, 1986; de Shazer, 1988). Now he has his frame, Don is able to go 'all out' on whatever is dissatisfying to Maja in the relationship; whatever these dissatisfactions are, they have been broken by a difference, admittedly small, about a year previously. This process is not one of 'pointing out positives' (usually an unproductive or even counterproductive process, as you have probably found in your own work); in response to the invitation to attend to exceptions, group members entertain new descriptions of themselves, others, and their relationships. The two descriptions are laid side by side, with the consultant maintaining an attitude of neutrality. . . . 'In this process, the therapist is not required to convince anyone of anything' (White, 1988, p. 8).

The drama can now be as 'big', flamboyant, or as small, pared-down, and precise as it needs to be. But whatever the style of the drama, its direction will always focus on the difference between the two stories, and the influence the problem has on her versus the influence she has on the problem. The direction is already established in 'real life' – it is from relatively poor communication with her mother to somewhat better communication, though still the subject of complaint. But even if the direction were opposite – from good to poor, the consultancy has a point of entry, a time when things changed, when a 'wedge' can be inserted. This point of change, for better or worse, provides the first tiny crack between the two types of description which can now be put side by side.

Don now tries to find another occasion when Maja experienced a difference in communication with her mother. He asks her to go back in time to when the relationship was more satisfactory. Together, they go down through Maja's life, starting from her present age – thirty-six – and heading backwards. Maja's first stop back down this road is when she was twenty – a time she became pregnant with her daughter. But the interaction with her mother is painful (same story), and Don asks her to choose an earlier period when things were somewhat better. Don and Maja keep going down the line. At each age that Maja stops, however, the interaction between mother and daughter is pained and blocked. At 14 and at 12 the relationship is still soured, and Don decides that he is not likely to get more exceptions (a time of blissful mother/daughter interaction, for example) by moving back any further.

Why is all this not more boring to the group? After all, so far you have not heard much about 'group process', the customary lubricant for social interest. The group is saved from boredom, and the leader saved from accusations of special treatment, by the fact that they are both essentially engaged in a *dramatic* process, low-key though it may be. Provided the timing is right and the theme is relevant to the group, the process will be of absorbing interest. You see, Don and Maja are not sitting in a circle, but are standing out in the front of the group on a 'stage' (though the stage is simply another part of the room). Despite the simplicity of the surroundings, each member of the group is nevertheless involved in the willing suspension of disbelief typical of the dramatic process; the flat floor has become a special area, where the realm of fantasy and that of 'reality' become blurred.

Don and Maja have now established a line that represents important periods in Maja's history of interaction with her mother. Each section of this line represents an age when a particular event occurred that is significant to Maja. Don and Maja do not only refer to these events, but they actually move around, and stand at particular points. A person from the group (called an 'auxiliary') has been chosen to be Maja's mother, and she stands on the line too. As you can gather, the staging for this drama is extremely stark: there are not even any props, such as chairs, which is rather uncommon. Maja is down to the bare dramatic essentials.

At each of the nominated periods in Maja's past, she and her mother engage in dialogue as if it were the present. In order that the auxiliary playing mother knows what to say, Maja and that person 'reverse roles'. Thus the dialogue is built up. This process has been described much more fully in *The Passionate Technique*, and the reader is advised to go to that book for more elaborate descriptions of full-length psychodramas. Here the focus is less on the mechanics of psychodrama than on the forbidden agendas that emerge in groups and individuals.

At twelve, Maja has her first period. She goes to her mother and tells her. Her mother says that she does not want to be bothered with such things – she has a farm to look after, a sick husband, and two other children, both boys. She indicates that there are some cloths in the cupboard, and dismisses the incident.

At fourteen, Maja becomes interested in a boy. She is confused by her experience, and wants to talk it over with her mother. The boy had come to the house, but was sent away by the parents. Maja's manner with her mother is tentative and fragile. Her mother says that she has no time for discussing these trifles, and that she should get on with her studies, and stop worrying. She ominously hints that 'things will happen' (meaning early pregnancy, or perhaps sinfulness at large) if she dallies with boys.

At sixteen, Maja is in boarding school. She has fallen in love with a lad. Her mother tells her that it is not for nothing that she has worked so hard on the farm to send her to school. She is terrified that Maja will leave her studies, and all her work to raise her for a better future than she herself had will come to nought.

Now the dialogue with the mother is more explicit. The hidden commands, rules, and fears become more transparent. Her own sacrifice is the one thing she trusts; it is her jewel, her truth – it is how she knows she loves someone. If her daughter will not make a similar sacrifice, perhaps that is a sign that she does not love her mother . . . even if Maja does not love her, she will continue to watch out for her best interests, continue to sacrifice, because that is the nature of love.

During this interaction, Maja goes into a kind of glazed-eyed trance; she loses her vitality, and does not know what to do.

This scene seems to suggest the crux of the matter: about the different ways one can love a person. Perhaps the craziest things, the grossest pathologies are manifestations of love – certainly, that is a widely held family-therapy view. The mother is demonstrating to Maja how much she loves her. This love consists of sacrifice, a prolonged caring, a seeing into the future, a wish that her daughter's life will transcend her own. Maja, on the other hand, is looking for a different kind of love – one based on the quick spirit, on vitality, and the direct sharing of inner experiences. In the drama, Maja is caught by her mother's gestalt, dulled and drugged by it. It is not a workable view for her; on the other hand, how can one shrug off love, how can one complain about it?

The mother weaves a web around Maja, binding her up: if she loves her mother, she will do what she says. Maja is transfixed by this web. She tries to burst out of it, but it is sticky. One can't burst out of a web – there is too much give. It is hard to fight, because it is all over one. The metaphor she has unconsciously chosen is realistic – her mother's love, her mother's culture, must always stay on her. At the same time, she can be relatively free of it. After a long struggle, she cleans off as many of the strands as she can, and faces her mother defiantly. Her face now shines with vitality and joy.

The next scene occurs when Maja is eighteen. She is much changed now – she seems lighter and freer. She has broken out of the paradox that to love is to curb the spirit. She says that she has 'many secrets' from her mother now. Don asks her what these secrets are. Maja giggles, and says they are too secret to tell. Obviously these secrets are a source of pride, rather than shame. She twirls around girlishly. Don asks whether anyone in the room speaks Czech. No one does. He asks Maja whether she would be prepared to say the secrets in Czech. She is delighted with this idea, and starts her narrative with her mother, covering her mouth with her hand, laughing and twirling after each one. Possibly these secrets are about romantic encounters that she has had, and she thinks these will shock her mother and the group.

She chooses the age of twenty as the next step in this saga. She tells her mother that she is pregnant. Her mother is horrified, and warns her of what this event will mean in terms of her interrupted education and future prospects. She says that it will be entirely Maja's responsibility to look after the child (although later, as it turns out, she becomes a doting and daily minding grandmother). Maja says that she does not care about all that, that she wants this child, and she is going to have it. Later, after the birth, she triumphantly presents her daughter to her mother (and thereby lowers her own risk of post-natal depression).

For the final scene, they move to the present. Don is now prepared to co-create some voluptuousness and the redress that is needed in the family legacy.

Maja, now herself an amusing, alert, and socially sensitive mother of a teenager, says that she wants to take her mother to a special place that 'women will enjoy'. They go to a luxurious spa. Maja points out proudly the deep soft towels, the thick robes, the perfumes and oils. Her mother, in role reversal, tut tuts at the waste. Maja calms her mother's fears, and urges her to enjoy the experience. They undress, and together sink into the warm perfumed water. They recline there, playing a little, chatting about this and that – inconsequential matters.

Then they talk more seriously about their different philosophies, and Maja explains that she does not have a philosophy of love through suffering, but one of love through joy. She has never worshipped sacrifice, she says, but judges according to what she can give, whether that is easy or hard. She rejoices in her own daughter's emerging sexuality, buys clothes with her, and tolerates the music. She wants her to live, to experience everything. She likes it that her daughter is growing up. She has come to this country because she had felt blocked and stuck in her mother (a slip?) country – here she enjoys the sunshine, the openness, the sensuality.

The drama ends with mother and daughter still in the spa, gazing at each other sometimes, but lightly, and recognizing a different person in there.

How is one to form an opinion on Don's consultancy? Certainly, he did not always behave as a typical psychodramatist. Except for the scene when Maja was sixteen and her mother had web-like ropes all over her, his 'hot' dramatization was minimal, consisting mostly of a walk through a kind of time line, with dialogue interspersed. And although much of the content seems to have been about sex, the issue of sex was not in itself explored psychodramatically. Did Don miss out on the link between Maja's sexuality and her mother's approval? Is Don a prude? A voyeur? Should he have gone to an early scene, where Maja's sexual identity was first formed, and have built up the scene psychodramatically? Even other scenes when she was twelve, fourteen, sixteen, eighteen, or twenty could have been developed with more dramatic impact, more ceremony, more careful staging. Should they have been?

Not necessarily. After all, this drama, like any story, can take dozens of different directions, being a co-creation of protagonist, director, and the group. Don was aiming to precipitate change by means of a process called 'double description'. He could have done this by more conventional means, such as by exploring Maja's childhood. In such an exploration, Don may have elected to put the story then – the text from the family of origin – beside any new story of Maja's choosing. At any stage of her life he could have found the relative influence (White, 1986) that she had over her problem versus the influence that the problem had over her. No matter how the enactment is styled – coarse, subtle, pathetic, angry, etc. (as often as not, more according to the predilections and level of psychological finesse of the director than those of the protagonist) – the point is first fully to engage, and then to separate Maja from her old story. In the second story, she can better experience her personal agency in a new description.

As it was, Don elected to make the double description concern difference from one time to another. He was looking for a point of 'leverage' where an exception to Maja's oppressive story presented itself. This exception contradicts the problem-saturated description that Maja presents of her relationship. Don can work outwards from that exception by comparing the points before and the point after the exception. Maja was enabled to notice the difference, and ultimately break from her performance of the first story.

Like many people in the grip of a problem, Maja thought that the problem was always there, and that it never changed:

> And precisely because the mind can receive news only of difference, there is a difficulty in discriminating between a *slow change* and a *state*. There is necessarily a threshold of gradient below which the gradient cannot be perceived.
>
> (Bateson, 1979, p. 109)

When nothing is different from anything else, people become stuck, because the mind can only receive (change by) perceptions of difference. Don first tried to accelerate time so that Maja's habituation to the problem was jolted. To distinguish between slow change and the unchanging, as Bateson says, we need a clock. Don's efforts were to put a clock in, so that the new was seen as new, and Maja could move on from there, and on from a simple redressive drama.

It is starting to sound as if Don's influence over the drama was univocal. Far from it. The very metaphor of 'binding' which Maja first brought up, and which Don shied away from because he was focusing on 'exceptions' at the time, was the one most fully dramatized. 'Warm-up will out', as any experienced therapist will tell you. In the long run, Maja did enact her scene for which she had 'act hunger'. And Don ultimately kept the drama focused on news of difference. It seems as if they both had a hand on the tiller, after all. Perhaps it is always so.

The low-key emotional tone was not the point: news of difference can as well be brought by mere suggestion and lightness of touch, as by the incandescent, sensual, or violent means of the full psychodramatic process. Provided the theoretical base for establishing information is present, Don and Maja could have got the same result from an exquisitely quiet enactment or by exuberantly hanging from the rafters. What matters is the framework of news of difference. At follow-up some months later, Maja had reoriented her relationship with her mother, was enjoying it more, and had noticed the changes continuing. Though doubtless some puzzles remained for her, she now told herself a new story about her relationship with her mum, and her mother told her a new one in turn.

Chapter two

Ideas for an outsider

The past is never dead. It is not even past.

William Faulkner

How things change; how they stay the same

Even trees respond to information. Tigers do, too, and so do elephants. Sunflowers turn their heads through the day, following the sun. A dog scratching its ear is responding to information – a real or imaginary bite by a flea, perhaps. Changes in living beings' systems are sometimes adaptations to the external environment – wet or dry, winter or summer, the presence of prey or food, an irritant such as a flea. At other times the information concerns internal functioning – hunger, let us say, or cold, or a wound. Whether the stimulus is internal or external, changes are not so much *imposed* from the outside as they are developed by the system as a response to information. The sun does not *make* the sunflower turn its head, the flea does not make the dog scratch, the wound does not make the blood cells rush to it.

All this may sound a little impersonal and irrelevant. After all, what has 'information' to do with the worm of pain that eats at our hearts? How does talk of sunflowers or elephants relate to the way problems oppress people or the emotional erosion they suffer? And how does bloodless information relate to a bright and carnal quality like spontaneity – that which Moreno (1953, p. 47) says we fear most of all? In this chapter I will suggest that 'information' is not so crusty; in the world of the living it is heart's blood itself. But sometimes that heart's blood no longer courses, and an outsider is called in to get the system going again. In the next few pages I will outline ways the 'outsider' can link information and story in drama so that the action becomes problem dis-solving. From the extended drama of Chapter 1 you may be used to a highly example-ridden style, and you could find that this chapter is a little different from the last, as it contains only two extended examples: 'Walking out' and 'Moira's armful'. Be prepared for the switch.

You would probably agree that people do take in some sorts of information and pass over others. This is why they can make sense of the same phenomena in astonishingly diverse ways – did you ever witness a car crash and hear the vastly different explanations of the two parties involved? We create the world that we perceive, not because there is no reality 'outside our heads', but because we select and edit reality to conform to our beliefs about what sort of world we live in (Bateson, 1972, p. vii). That is pretty strong: as well as perceptions determining beliefs, then (we are accustomed enough to that idea), it could be said that beliefs determine perceptions. A simple example may tempt you to consider this position: if you are a fan of one football club, you will not only interpret actions on the field differently from a fan of the rival club, you will actually *see* different things happening on the field. Your beliefs about the rightness of your club's actions will act as a template over your perceptions about what really does go on on that grass.

Sometimes changes in the external environment or internal functioning necessitate action to which the system immediately responds – we are hot, so we sweat; we are cold, so we shiver. Much of this goes on smoothly and autonomously; the processes are unconscious, economical, and habitual. The conscious organism does not need to know *how* it perceives – only to know *what* it perceives. Imagine the clutter in our consciousness if we had to 'tell' our heart to beat each time, to monitor our digestion, the growth of cells, our cooling and warming systems, and even to direct each stage of mending that little cut on our hand. The information that 'tells' us to sweat or to shiver is outside our perception. In fact, it is inaccessible to perception.

In social interaction, too, we often cannot tell why we did something – what invisible rule or norm we were following, what nuance of social command or cry from the other we were picking up. We are regulated by habit and pattern here, too, much of which is outside our perception. I am suggesting that 'information' for us humans takes place on two levels – the level of automatic and biological response – so we breathe when we need to, and scratch our head without thinking if we feel an itch. But other information, social information, becomes *story*; we connect events in time and give them a meaning or interpretation. These meanings are then used to frame further events. It is with this type of information that the consultant, and therefore this book, is concerned. All of us, groups and organizations too, run by story. We know anything, even our happiness, even 'what happened', by selection and editing of reality 'out there'. Mostly the process is inadvertent, and even when destructive, done with the best of intentions. When people make themselves and others unhappy, they are not being so much illogical as logically following poor maps very carefully.

We do not edit reality all on our own; culture also has its pattern books and censor's shears. Human groups – such as families, schools, offices, or clubs – rely on their current pattern of organization to respond to changes in the environment. Ways that have proved adaptive in the past are preserved, like fruit in marmalade, in norms, beliefs, and values. Moreno called this preservation of beliefs the 'cultural conserve'. This social marmalade can exist at a minor level, such as in a family or a group, or at the larger level of culture itself. Culture – and groups – run by a pattern of basic and often unstated assumptions that have worked well enough to be considered valid, and which are taught to new members as the correct way to view their problems. The assumptions change over time, and become more embedded into the out-of-awareness functioning of the group – that is, the group culture is conserved more and more unconsciously. Well, if conservation is the means by which things stay the same, how do things change?

The outsider

Firstly, change can come by someone simply doing something different – by a miracle called 'spontaneity' – which breaks the clutch of the conserve. Conserved patterns of perceiving are only problematic when difficulties arise, and even then we may be able to do something different. We are locked in an argument, so we start laughing, or go to the pictures. When someone breaks clear of what is already known, safe, and predictable, they force a reorganization of the system around them. They spontaneously create a new organization that works better than the preceding one.

When social interaction does not work so well, an outsider is sometimes called in. Alas, one's troubles are not yet over. Any living system will take in what is compatible or seems nourishing, but throw out that which is foreign to it, or is not seen as useful. Living systems generally suspect what they do not recognize, and this includes 'outsiders' trying to change it. This means you, Reader; and me, too. We will reject the 'outside' information or interventions just as a body rejects a splinter. As the splinter is not recognized as fitting with the finger as the finger knows itself, so pus forms around it to take it away. Like the splinter, 'perfectly good advice' is squeezed out or ignored; if we were to be honest, we could find many instances when we have done the same. The advice might be fine, but, somehow, we just cannot take it on board. Even the very sound advice we give to ourselves – to stop smoking, take more exercise, not to quarrel so much, etc., may fall on deaf ears – our own. Somehow we are as prevented from taking our own good counsel as we are the advice of others.

It is as if people (we) are *restrained* from taking alternative courses, even when these courses seem most sensible. The information somehow does not manage to inform us. Though one's present pattern of behaviour is unsatisfactory, yet one acts as if the options were limited or non-existent. The restraints are not absolute, of course; they are factors which Bateson (1972, p. 399) says determine 'inequality of probability'. (In simpler terms, you can still play, but the dice are loaded.) Restraints establish the rules for selection of information about people or events; they are a template that fits over everything we experience. They stop information from informing us; though the information is 'there', we are not ready to 'hear'.

Outsiders (directors, consultants, therapists) try to unload the dice. They ready people for the selection of new ideas. How is this done? Certainly not by pushing, but by easing the restraints. You see, they cannot actually give the new ideas until the system is ready to receive. Living systems (us), as you know, completely regulate themselves by information. Our sense organs can receive *only* news of difference, which must be coded into events in time (that is, changes) in order to be perceptible. Ordinary static differences that remain constant for more than a few seconds require us to be active in order to know them. We must scan them – that is, move our eye from one to the other – or bring together observations from separated moments. You cannot see anything in a whiteout – there are no distinctions, and consequently it is not safe to move.

When clients' problems are those of 'whiteout' or inadequate distinctions, they will read their story, the text of which is something like 'I am anxious' or 'I am depressed'. It is only when one asks them to read the text a little more closely that one finds that this depression or anxiety had a beginning; that they were not always equally depressed, but that some days are worse than others, and some hours worse than others; that at the onset of 'the depression' several major unpleasant events had occurred. Perhaps even that the depression was a way of keeping someone else from worrying about *their* troubles, and so on. Even such a simple thing as news of difference about the depression itself (for example, when they are depressed, when they are not) can create helpful distinctions, and enable the composition of a life text that is fuller and freer.

In terms of consultancy, the outsider must first of all be recognized as 'not foreign'. This means that at the outset, they join fully with the first description, so that the system recognizes the outsider as someone who will not have to be thrown out. With the system's identity (whether it be a single person, a dyad, or a group) no longer at risk, indeed confirmed, it can play with the new. Directors attempt to get a deep engagement with the old story, with the 'what is' of the complaint. In psychodramatic terms, this deep engagement is called 'warm-up'.

Warming up to a role

Warming up to a role, and the continuous unfolding of roles, is a somewhat more technical meaning of warm-up than the more easily comprehended notion of 'group starters', which will be the focus of Chapter 6. It may already make sense to you, though, to speak of directors 'warming themselves up to the role of leading the group', or of protagonists being 'warmed up to the group' and the group being warmed up to them. After a session starts, one might speak of protagonists being fully warmed up to the roles they are enacting; they go through roles and become ready for others like snakes shedding various layers of skin. The notion is not restricted to action methods or therapy – by rights it refers to a process in life, too.

Walking out

Max, a psychiatric nurse, has been in a therapy group for six sessions, where his behaviour alternates between gloomy silence or endlessly holding the floor with what the group complains of as irrelevant detail. Many of his statements appear to be grandiose, and unfounded on his being as he presents himself; when challenged, he either flies into a rage or cocoons himself in misery, staring at his feet.

One night he seems different, more direct and present. Delia has been warming up the group by asking people to share their awareness of what they do and how they experience themselves (we shall see some of the pitfalls of even this innocent method when we discuss Dorrie's group in the chapter on 'Warm-up to what?'). Delia promotes crossfire, listens empathically, and leads as quickly as possible to enactment.

It is clear that the group has begun to focus on Max, listening to him for the first time not as unwilling prisoners of his monologues or as indulgent parents whose duty it is to draw him out. For reasons that are for the moment mysterious, he has become the sociometric star (see later chapters) of the group, and has succeeded in the first steps of warming them up to himself. Delia now attempts to warm him up more fully to some of his major roles.

D: *Max, would you be willing to put out what's going on for you now?*
Max: *I want to loosen up a bit, make friends with people. I'm lonely, see, but I like it that way. There's no one on the same level. Everyone round here is so superficial. . . . Ah, it's just hopeless. . . . When*

> *I'm working, I don't miss people too much. I have such a lot of responsibility. . . . Give, give, give, that's me. My nightmare is ordinary nights; even though I do extra work most nights at the hospital, I still have to go home sometime. (He falls into a mournful silence. Hunched and temporarily humbled, he stares at his shoes.)*

Delia decides that she will not ask Max her usual questions (see 'Interviewing for a role' in The Passionate Technique*) about with whom he would like to be more friendly, how he would know if he were getting somewhere with this problem, etc. She also reflects that if she were to ask Max to set up his 'nightmare' at this stage, he would lose face and she would lose him. Instead, she determines to use the impetus that got him to speak to her in the first place, and to continue his warm-up to more functional roles by means of direct action. She says to him:*

Don't worry about talking to me for the moment. I see you're looking at your shoes. Watch them move. Walk and soliloquize. Speak out loud what's going on inside. As you do so, you'll generate some ideas. . . .

Ah, I see that you walk in a very determined manner; this will be a great asset to you in this session. But it also seems from your walk that you find difficulty in contacting the little child, the tender part of you. This must be experienced as quite a loss to you, eh? (his face softens, then sets again even more resolutely than before). (Hastily, realizing her error of timing) Keep on walking. Be determined. Leave no stone unturned in your efforts to get the perfect determined walk. A walk that lets people know that you mean business. Martine, come out for a minute and double Max; help him get into it.

Like any segment of group leadership, Delia's can be questioned, especially regarding the validity of this form of warming up, and the direction of change that is likely to eventuate. Some of you might see Delia as acting with the highest possible skill – adroit, flexible, carefully tracking, joining, and spontaneous herself. Others will conclude that her work will lead to nothing but void excitement and increasing dependency on the group to give a 'charge'. Vitalism, no matter how skilfully evoked, goes nowhere if the director has nothing more in mind than to get the protagonist or the group to a pitch of excitement which is later 'resolved' by action.

Let me put the psychodrama case: in groups based on action methods, the warming-up process consists of getting a person or the whole group 'warm' to feel, think, and act in new ways. It starts with arousal to a theme, for example 'my eating habits' or 'me as an efficient manager', and leads to accessing certain roles. Even these roles may be only transitional – say, comic, violent, or apparently hysterical – but they serve the purpose of moving the person on to other more functional roles that are the real point of the process. Max must fully enact his 'first story'; that is, he warms up to the role of 'Defiant Isolate', let us say, before any other story is open to him. By Delia joining with his first story, Max is able to access it more fully himself. The purpose of the transitional role states (walking determinedly, in this case) is ultimately to warm the person up to the functional roles that are adequate to the real-life situation.

Joining with the first story is like someone setting up a password at the sentry post: on hearing the correct words, the sentry says 'Enter'. The password is the first story, not disputed – elaborated even, if the director decides to come on strong and enact it. There cannot be an acceptance of new ideas until the old ideas are accepted. It is best if this process is surprisingly thorough – maybe not even the clients accept the old description as fully as the consultant does. As often as not, the first description has been only a rough sketch, the lines of which have been in lunatic fashion gone over and over so often, that they are scored deep in the paper. We can betray ourselves by the simplest ideas, said often enough. Even to present this old description thoroughly, painting it in fully, taking care of the detail and the shadings is, of course, a kind of second description already. Simply by describing itself more fully, a system can change.

But not always. When the first story is presented as fully as need be, the second can be laid alongside, forming a 'double description'. Clients are then asked to compare the two, and to see which of them suits his or her sort of person best. This comparison of the two is sometimes involuntary and automatic, while at other times it requires a careful side-by-side comparison over time. Using two scene set-ups on the stage, they may flick from one to the other, so that the learning is visceral, visual, and vocal. 'What feeds, what starves this problem?' asks the outsider, and the protagonist sets up and enacts a feeding/starving dialectic. The type of learning here can go very deep, because the mode is not merely verbal: the dramatic fully serves a 'strategic' orientation.

Whatever the actual format, the skilled outsider tries to dig gutters so that the old information ('You are no good'; 'It is dangerous to stop quarrelling', etc.) can drain away, and to make little fountains so that new information can trickle in. For example, if an adolescent suddenly leaves home, that same act can be storyed as one of rebellious vindictiveness (old description) or a wonderful gesture of independence and initiative (new description). 'Rebellious vindictiveness' and 'a wonderful sense of independence', of course, are only two of the infinite number of stories that can be told about what that person is doing. When they have been placed side by side to form a double description, the family can be asked which description they prefer. They can hop from side to side to get a 'feel' for each position; they can see what they have been doing, and must do, to maintain each position.

Metaphors: information-bearers and information-hiders

Flaubert complained of being bothered by his tendency to metaphor – 'I am devoured by them as one is by lice, and I spend my time doing nothing but squashing them.' He is not the only one. Continually casting our senses into experience, we reel in contrasts and affinities that become what we 'know'. The contrasts are called 'differences', and the intimate or obvious affinities are called 'metaphors'. Metaphors offer almost irresistible enticements in action groups: placing a decent metaphor near a director is like flicking a fly near a trout, or a whisky near an alcoholic. After all, why should directors not be tempted? Images are where the action is – they hold the colour and the life; from image to its incarnation is such a short and so gratifying a step for the experienced action worker.

Perhaps I should not have tempted you with Flaubert's lice, or with flies and whisky. These are *overt* metaphors (or similes, or analogies – do you mind if I lump them all in the pot so that we can just say 'stew' without nominating the ingredients each time?). Overt metaphors are those most often used in action methods – 'this family is a *sewer*'; 'there's just a *brick wall* between my husband and me'; 'it will be just *heaven* to get this company wound up'. Directors are not slow to ask the protagonists to set up sewers, brick walls, and heavens, given this succulent bait.

There is more to the director's process, one hopes, than the desire for some colour and movement, entrancing though these may be. You would rightly view Flaubert's lice or my fly as a specific contrivance, an intentional juxtaposing to one experience the properties of another. *Covert* metaphors, however, are not so recognizable, literary, or witting. They occur accidentally, as it were, in our personal and cultural language, and we are relatively unconscious of making them up. It is just the way we think. Maybe it comes right down to base level: we know anything because of like and unlike – the links that we agree on making up. We concur in linking things, too – this is a chair because it is like other things (called chairs) and unlike yet others – pembrokes, newfoundland hounds, or celestial beings (called tables, dogs, and angels, respectively).

This is not just a game. The type of metaphors we use becomes highly important at the behavioural level. Lakoff and Johnson (1980) give some examples which show how metaphors actually direct thinking. I will take only three from their series on love:

Love is madness

I'm *crazy* about her. She *drives me out of my mind*. He constantly *raves* about her. He's gone *mad* over her. I'm just *wild* about Harry. I'm *insane* about her.

Love is magic

She *cast her spell* over me. The *magic* is gone. I was *spellbound*. She had me *hypnotized*. I was *entranced* by him. I'm *charmed* by her. She is *bewitching*.

Love is a war

He is known for his many rapid *conquests*. She *fought for* him, but his mistress *won out*. He *fled from her advances*. She *pursued him relentlessly*. He is slowly *gaining ground* with her. He *won* her hand in marriage. He *overpowered* her. She is *besieged* by suitors. He has to *fend them off*. He *enlisted the aid* of her friends. He *made an ally* of her mother. Theirs is a *misalliance* if ever I've seen one.

You can see how if you held one metaphor or another you would dramatically affect your beloved and the people around you. These or similar ways of talking are not poesy or rhetoric; they are deep within culture and are, anyway, all that we have. Metaphors not only allow us to perceive resemblances that had previously gone unnoticed, but can also be the means whereby psychic realities are created in the first place. They extend the reach of speech, and allow the speaker unconventional experience of the conventionally known (Arcaya, 1985, p. 22). To this extent one might say that they are 'information-bearers'. Our constructions of the world, suggest Lakoff and Johnson (1980), emerge from our interaction with it, which starts off as limited and physical. We can only reach out further by abstraction of similarities.

We define our reality in terms of metaphors and then proceed to act on their basis as if they were the reality itself. But by highlighting certain features of experience, metaphors automatically shade other features, and thereby limit behaviour. That gives them potential to be 'information-hiders' as well as 'information-bearers'. All behaviour is limited in one way or another, of course, but sometimes it is unhelpfully narrow. The important metaphorical constructions that are the subject of consultancy tend to operate in clusters, so that an entire domain of experience is structured in terms of another domain. A person who operates on the image that 'one must have goals in life or one will get nowhere', for example, will experience 'reality' differently from someone who thinks that life is 'a garden' or 'a journey to heaven' or 'a desert'. Whether one regards love as magic, war, or madness, and life as a garden, a journey, or a desert can matter quite deeply.

Consultants try to find the domain from which the comparison is drawn, and what other one or ones would be helpful – to replace the old story, constructed out of one or a cluster of metaphors, with the new. They create news of difference by bringing two metaphors side by side, and allowing the new ones to take the weight for a while. They hope that group members will be able to select the second lot as being more serviceable, and that the new information-bearing stumps will outlast the old ones, good in their day, perhaps, but which now have dry rot. There is no 'getting rid of' metaphor – there is only replacement.

In summary, metaphor is not a decoration of language, but the beginning of thought itself, if you regard 'thinking' as the ability to perceive and identify new relationships. That is why action methods devote time and space to elaborating a story: the process in itself is likely to lead to new connections. These new connections are not only intellectual: our glories and our problems are at base interpersonal, and spontaneity itself is not an abstract process, but a product – and sometimes – a casualty of human attachments.

Co-creation

Externalization is more usually called 'concretization' in the psychodrama literature. The term is sometimes deliberately interchanged here to link it to systems theory. Some of you may think that systems theory and psychodrama have not even been introduced, far less be in a state to contemplate progeny. But in fact Moreno for his day was an advanced systems thinker (Campernolle, 1981), and some of his ideas pre-dated modern cybernetic theory. The mating of systems theory and action methods (Strategic Action Consultancy) may be able to provide you with a cybernetic theory suitable for use in groupwork. Since the only way we know anything, including how to get out of trouble, is by difference, it is sensible directly to use processes most likely to bring news of difference.

Words like 'cybernetic' are formidable and not at all attractive. Often they boil down to the simplest ideas, but, because they go against the way we usually think, they seem difficult and contrary. 'Second-order cybernetics' (even more formidable-sounding and less attractive) means not much more than acknowledging the part that the observer plays in any system. The concept is important to group leaders, despite the awkwardness of the term: for example, even if consultants are in a system only for a short time, and to do a specific job, they cannot escape being part of the system. Anyone working on or even observing a system affects that system, is affected by it, and in fact constitutes a new system. Objectivity is a false and protective hope in consultancy, right from the briefing stage.

All is not lost: leaders, like family members, like anyone else who wants something different to happen within their system, have to change it by their own spontaneity and skill at being themselves. On their side, one hopes, they also have the role of expertness, and perhaps the experience of having been in this situation before. Strictly speaking, there is no such thing as 'the group' and 'the leader' (though each has different roles, tasks, and levels of experience). To be accurate, one must refer to the 'group/leader system', but no one wants to go around using language like that, I think. The group, and all that happens in it, is a 'co-creation' of director and members.

D: What's happening to you now, Marge, as Mick speaks to you?
M1: I'd like the limelight to be off. I'd like this thing to be over.
D: Express yourself now, Mary – what's that face all about?
M2: I think Mick is being hurt.
M1: (to Mick) I'm scared of being your friend.
M3: (to Mick) Why don't you have the same generosity to me, Mick?
M1: (shouts) Because you fuck me around!
D: It seems like there is something going on about being included.
M4: (interrupts) I'm not Mick!
D: (valiantly) Marge, would you be willing to put out what's going on for you now.
M1: I feel inadequate in relationships. The ordinary things I assume go on just don't. The whole business of people getting on with others is just beyond me. I don't want to get chopped up. . . .

How far is the director in on all this? Up to her neck, surely. The material 'uncovered' in consultation and therapy – even in the first story – is creative constructions rather than objective discoveries. That is what makes acting on a metaphor so legitimate – the reality is obviously 'cooked up' by both of them. The new reality cannot be too new, however. An 'as if' fiction will only be acceptable if it fits the language and framework already being used. The aim of consultancy can thus never be to discover 'real' reality; the quest has to be the somewhat modest one of constructing a more appropriate reality. The protagonist works through a first story which might (as in 'Moira's armful', below) be the simple elaboration of a metaphor, and then in surplus reality reconstructs a new text (often called 'insight' in the language of traditional therapy) which the protagonist regards as 'true' or more appropriate.

Moira's armful

Moira complains that she is always 'taking on things in a spirit of generosity, and then getting dumped'. She tells of an international seminar she had recently managed where she had started as part of the organizing committee and ended up with nearly all the work as people reneged for family reasons or because they had 'higher' things to do.

Duke asks her to pick up a chair (they were not the stackable variety, mind) for every duty that she picked up on the committee, and to walk towards the stage, where the drama will begin. Moira accepts this task willingly. She begins to pick up chairs, one, two, three, four. Somehow she stacks these four under her arm, and begins to snatch up two more with her left hand. By this time she is staggering like a poisoned giraffe, and on one occasion drops the lot. Patiently, she starts again.

The absurdity of what she is doing does not strike her. She is covered in chairs, invisible behind them, but struggles on towards the stage. She drops all the chairs again. Duke asks her to pick them up once more. She begins to do so, then suddenly throws them down, unable to believe that she has been so foolish.

At last (with three-quarters of the drama over) she reaches the stage. Duke asks her to select from the group people to represent the committee members who had reneged on their duties. At first reluctantly, then with more gusto, she confronts each of them. She throws a now-hated chair back into each one's hands. 'It's like being the unmarried daughter in a family', she says. 'You just exploit me. You think my life is worth nothing because I haven't got children. And I swallowed it! I helped you do this to me! Well no more. No more.' She continues in this vein for some time, picking chairs up and furiously pressing them into the auxiliaries.

This drama was followed up a few days later, and then two months later. Moira reported significant changes in her life: she claimed to be much more comfortable with herself, and felt confident about what she was doing. She had successfully confronted in real life every member of the committee that she had confronted in the drama. 'I saw Toby, for example, and I could say what I wanted to say to him and just leave it. The interactions were so clear – they started, they stopped. I did not do any explaining and justifying.' About another member: 'I just saw what she was doing and smiled.' Furthermore, that direct and simple way of being seemed to have generalized: she was not compulsively taking on so many obligations, and was doing what she did do with less resentment. There was another pay-off, too, all these months later: not only did she feel more in charge of her life, but people actually seemed to like her more.

In the analogical task ('before we begin the drama') of picking up the chairs to represent commitments, Moira has acted a very powerful metaphor for herself. This was the first story, the first description. The director helps her warm up fully to this first description, joining her system at her system's own level of narrative, and making use of a dramatic analogue (chairs) to extend that first description. Duke knows full well that this is not objective truth they are uncovering – that attempts to exhume the 'really real' are futile, no matter how careful a 'history' is taken. Of course, the narrative produced in a particular session is neither a repetition nor a distortion of what actually occurred, but itself a construct – a creation between the member and the leader, which they build together. It is, in the truest sense, a fabrication, but in no way a lie. Not only the 'second story' is built in what psychodramatists call 'surplus reality'; so is the first.

Moira acts her second story when she thrust the chairs into the auxiliaries' hands. She has thus created two versions of reality, or a 'double description', and could make a visceral choice of which one she preferred. Obviously it was the second. She re-describes herself as a putting-things-back-in-people's-hands sort of person, rather than an 'unmarried-daughter-who-must-take-on-everything-because-she-has-nothing-better-to-do' sort of person.

In groups, people sometimes act as if they were following another agenda altogether, an agenda forbidden to be spoken of, forbidden even to be known to the people who follow it. One of Bion's (1961) great contributions to understanding groups was to show that the whole group, by acting on these agendas, unconsciously created metaphors which evaded the real purpose of the group. (Bion settled on three basic metaphors – 'fight/flight', 'dependency', and 'pairing', and called them 'Basic Assumptions'.) I am calling 'forbidden agendas' those restraints on seeing reality differently: some are born in the group of alliances and coalitions, and some are brought with people when they enter the group.

Most of the examples in the first part of the book will concern the elasticizing of restraints on descriptions that people bring, almost ready-made, to the group. So although Maja (see Chapter 1) warmed up to difficulties with her mum in the group context, the restraints on how she saw her relationship with her mother had long been operating. Group and 'back home' interact. Similarly, the restraints preventing Moira from seeing that she had alternative roles to 'unmarried daughter' in her community were lifted so that she could entertain a new description of herself. Examples in subsequent chapters (especially 'Warm-up to what?' and 'Strategic sociometry') will elaborate at greater length the group forbidden agendas.

Chapter three

Social atom and self

The truth isn't always beauty, but the hunger for it is.

Nadine Gordimer

Social atom

Action methods and psychodrama are popularly associated with an heroic but naive individualism: somewhat vaguely, people lump them together with the culture of the 1960s and the 'me generation' that followed it. Now it is quite true that Moreno attempted to evoke the 'total subjectivity' and 'megalomania normalis' of the individual; but he also well understood that our social world – our 'social atom' as he called it – was essential to well-being.

Social atoms are the 'smallest functional unit within the social group' (Moreno, 1953, p. 69); they consist of each individual's link-up with others – family, friends, school, work, and so on. The unfamiliar terminology – such as 'protagonist', 'catharsis', 'tele', and 'megalomania normalis' – comes from Moreno's fondness for using words by early philosophers and dramatists, especially Greek; he liked what he called their 'poetic-symbolic character'. Though the name 'social atom' may seem a little strange, the concept is an easy enough one to grasp: imagine that around every individual are spinning circles of relationships, thicker around some people, thinner around others. Each person's circle is their social atom.

In this chapter I want to suggest some new domains of working with groups based on conceptions of 'me' and 'us' which lead from the notion of dialectic to that of relative autonomy. If you are an experienced groupworker or psychodrama trooper, you can expect some disappointments: many of the examples on offer may seem a bit 'old hat'. Please forgive me; I am not always suggesting a new way of doing something so much as a new way of knowing what you are doing – a framework for action as against trying something that you have seen before because it seemed to 'work'. Not that anything should be condemned just because it 'works'. On the contrary. But it is handy to have a way of varying things when they go wrong, and a theory can sometimes help with that.

Many psychological workers prefer to see people in groups rather than individually because a group becomes a mini- (and temporary) social atom within which experimentation can occur. Social atoms, whether a temporary group, one's family, one's friendship circle, one's job, or the mix of all of these, are constituted by a flow of feeling, to and fro. I always think of the basic social atom as a kind of street directory, a map of our social relationships as they stand at the moment. The exercise associated with it is familiar to most people who have tried any form of action methods:

Stand in a particular spot in the room. Now, using other people as auxiliaries, place them near or far to you according to their emotional distance at this moment. You can also have 'things' in it like your job, your dog, your church, this group, or whatever. Put in whatever is most important to you.

The process that attracts individuals to one another or which repels them, the flow of feelings of which social atoms are composed, is called 'tele'. It was not only the methods of Freud's 'talking cure' that Moreno disparaged; he was also against over-individualistic therapies that treated a person as a unit with 'micro-cosmic independence'. He liked concepts that we today would call 'Mind' – the pattern that connects. Tele is one such instance: tele is the relationship itself; it does not reside in a single individual, or spring from one person exclusively. Such thinking was considered (Moreno, 1953. p. 54) evidence of a 'materialistic' concept of an individual. So a social atom was construed almost as something outside an individual, in which relationships between people 'resided'. Cybernetic theorists would approve this as a more complete way of describing an individual: a 'triple description' – first of one person's roles, then of the other's, and culminating in a description of the system between them. The system between them is almost a third party, one might say.

'Social atom' and 'tele' are further evidence of Moreno's strongly interpersonal notion of a self: a self is always in relationship, and is made whole by improved relationships. Moreno wanted to develop a therapy based on the affinities among people and the patterns resulting from their spontaneous interactions. Such a therapy would centre on the idea of leaving the individual unchanged, or changed 'only so far as this is bound to occur through the reorganization of groupings' (1953, p. 5). He did not favour an analysis 'backward towards the past trauma', but thought that help would come through 'the training of the individual's spontaneity based on the analysis of present performance'. Ironically enough,

Moreno's systemic and sociometric emphasis on present interactions maintaining the problem has been all but lost. His fame now resides in psychodrama, which in the last twenty years of his life, and until now, has been highly oriented towards 'past trauma'.

There is nothing amiss with going back into the past, if that is helpful. A strategic worker will go anywhere there is leverage. Whether past or present, the interest of a strategic action consultant lies in the world of difference or distinction. So let us put a simple cybernetic twist on the conventional social atom presentation. In addition to the exercise represented a few moments ago, you can do a comparison with yourself at a year ago, or ten years, or however long you like:

Leaving that first social atom of 'you now' still set up, do a similar exercise with yourself two years ago. Put in all the people or organizations that are important two years ago. Place them near or far according to their emotional distance to you.

This time, you have laid out one description, and then followed it up with a second, so forming a 'double description' – me now and me then. If you were being directed, the director could then ask you to comment on the two, and the differences between them. Now the differences are coded into changes, or 'events in time' as Bateson (1979) would call them. You can then speak from one time to another, for instance, or you can set up the events that led to these changes in the social atom. What people are new? Who has changed places? What is the shape of each atom and why are they different? Maybe there was a single event – a marriage, a betrayal, an illness, a birth, a death – that was pivotal in the changed shape of the social atom. This event can then be acted out, as can systemic restraints and rewards in the future.

Go to a year in the future. Imagine that you have made the changes that you have come into this group to make. Set up your social atom in the way it will have rearranged itself when you have made these changes. What are the negative effects of your changing?

By expressing the implicit and hidden forces forbidding change, and the negative reactions to the protagonist becoming any different, directors allow clients to experience the systemic restraints against change. They become fully involved with the social conditions under which they have little chance of achieving what they want to achieve. By proceeding in this fashion, a director has flexibility to work with the restraints on change within the group, the here-and-now social atom, or within the person's back-home social atom.

A 'group' provides a temporary social atom in itself, and an action methods group has the added advantage of being able to represent physically significant others in an individual's or organization's life. One's family members can be represented, or the boss, or the organization, or 'the whole world', if one wishes. Difficulties may have been experienced because of not enough distinction between the self and other – 'enmeshment', or because there is too much distance – 'disengagement'. Action methods provide physical means, through their use of space, to modulate and understand this self/other distance. The interpersonal context of the self, furthermore, can refer to the present group or to each person's wider social world. Herein lies the advantage of the method: while it is quite possible that dilemmas associated with self/other will be replayed in a group setting, to limit people's work in a group only to refer to the members of 'this group' tends to make the group intensely self-absorbed in a way that is not always helpful. On the other hand, it is wise at times to steer interactions back into the here-and-now of the group so that the learning does not only stay at an intellectual level.

I have been suggesting in the chapters leading up to this that the problems that people bring, and for which they are in 'a group' in the first place, are the result of their organizing their lives around certain stories and meanings. Unfortunately, these stories often contribute to the survival of the very problem for which they seek help. The question becomes: how does one help people to create new meanings which no longer contribute to the survival of the problem? It is not enough simply to 'give' the new story – it has to be taken in as part of the client's meaning-structure which itself always exists in an interpersonal context.

You will understand that the story that we have is not ours alone, but has been co-created by others in our social environment. Even the new story (if we are lucky enough to get one from our own resources or from therapy) does not belong to us exclusively – our autonomy is only ever relative. Maybe this is not so disappointing after all: Nietzschean absolute autonomy – the psychocultural dream of the sixties – is perhaps a rather chilling concept anyway. At least relative autonomy – partial freedom from one's original system – is a long way preferable to being swamped by problem-saturated obligations and 'invisible loyalties' that do neither us nor others any good. Loyalties are an inevitable and perhaps one of the finest parts of being human; it is only sometimes that their effect is dysfunctional, creating forbidden agendas in the form of restraints.

What does all this mean in practice? In practice, consultants have to deal with a primary dialectic between self and other. All of us strive for relatedness to other human beings, and at the same time feel the need to move away to develop a personal identity. On the one hand, we experience ourselves as unique, distinct, and significant; on the other, it is clear that we need to be part of a network of familiar, nurturing, and sustaining others who are quite reliably connected to us. In a group, as in life, this problem continues: how to maintain a balance between the self's stability and cohesion, and being open to new experience which might run the risk of shattering it?

The me/us dialectic, though subjectively experienced as discomfort and tension, nevertheless provides ready-made prospects for triggering spontaneity. In dialectical thinking, a 'self' cannot be treated as an absolute: it is always related to 'other'. The dialogue between self and other – whether the 'other' is another person, a part of oneself, a problem, an organization, or one's mum, is the very basis of action methods. Our struggle to stay lively is helped if someone else reflects our reality back to us in images of motion and change, presenting to us the contradictory and ephemeral nature of our reality. Action methods have a head-start here, because in drama everything is on the move anyway; drama by its nature works up the contradictions in the stories we tell ourselves – our own mixture of insecurity and resolve, guilt and pride, selfishness and compassion.

Applications: populating the action

The way people speak and act is the way they define their lives. That lives are lived as narrative and story becomes abundantly clear in action methods. So is the way one person's story is plaited with the stories of others: there *is* no detectable single strand that can be followed from beginning to end. It keeps disappearing into the rope – the story of the family, the story of culture itself. Sometimes the concept 'individual therapy' seems like madness, but it could be that no one really does it anyway. How could they, when not only the stories of client and significant others have always been plaited, but even the stories of therapist and client start to interweave from the first interview?

The bound-upness of other people's story with an individual's problem-saturated narrative (i.e. the systemic nature of difficulties) is most obvious in action consultancy when the dramas overtly concern family-of-origin issues, or current social atom events. In the course of an enactment it is not difficult to elicit (or create) the interpersonal nature of a thought, a feeling, or a behaviour. Dramatic externalization allows one to see how the problem could not survive if the system were not as it is. Change the system, change the problem; or, if you like to do things the hard way, change the problem and you change the system (though the system might do its best to change back again). Nevertheless, if systems are true ecologies, change anywhere in the system means changing the whole system.

From the systemic point of view, then, not to mention that of aesthetics, it is preferable to keep short the 'intrapsychic' phase of any interaction (I talk to a 'part' of myself). At best, the intrapsychic phase is a warm-up to actually populating the stage with figures from the protagonist's social atom. (Jungians would say these are only archetypes anyway – that everyone 'outside' is really only a projection of someone 'inside'. With modifications, this view would not be too much at odds with the constructivist position taken in this book.) Endless dialogues between people and their 'anger', their 'fear', or their 'groundedness' make for tedious, messy drama and poor systemic thinking on the part of protagonist and group. They may be valid enough places to start a systemic enactment, but if extended too far can become problem-producing therapy that canonizes stuck beliefs.

To be sure, group members most often lead out with a problem-saturated statement about the self and a 'state' of the self: 'I am afraid'; 'my anger'; 'my procrastination'. The director may well externalize that, and then keep moving so that the inner dialogue is eventually externalized, not as two parts of the self, but as self and other. For example, Miro has said that he is 'confused':

D: Choose someone and place them in the chair to represent 'You who are confused'. (Miro does so.) Select someone to be your mother and have her stand beside the chair. (Miro does so.) Now select someone to be your father, and have them stand the other side. (He does so.) Now reverse roles with your father. . . .
Father, have a discussion with your wife about Miro's confusion. . . . Reverse roles with your mother (Miro does so). Interact with your husband, Mother. . . . (does so – they talk for a few moments). . . . Now direct a remark to your son about his confusion.

The director probably made a therapeutic guess here, and actually chose the discussants in this very obviously co-created vignette. But at least it is an illustration that the conversations we have with ourselves can be transformed into fuller roles, the fragments into a continuing dialogue with other people. Self-talk, including 'being confused', is part of our evolving story about ourselves, operating like film clips from the past: 'speakers' from our history, perhaps admonishing us, or encouraging us to take certain actions or to censor certain impulses. The most 'inner' voice is ultimately interpersonal; the most private dialogue is ultimately social. In the example outlined above, the inner dialogue is crudely extended to encompass people from the protagonist's original social atom. The director rapidly sets up a family-of-origin *system* around Miro's confusion. Notice that Miro is restrained from entering the interaction until the Mother/Father dialogue is well established.

His 'confusion', for which there is no referent given or sought, is contextualized as part of a family-of-origin triangle. This technique is very powerful, and is reinforced by the social influence process operating between consultant and client, director and protagonist. A protagonist will tend to follow the lead as if the director knows absolutely what he or she is doing. But stories offered by the director can canonize a point of view that is not necessarily in the person's interests. It can suggest that everything about which Miro is unhappy is ultimately attributable to mum and dad.

At a less flashy level, one does not have to look far to facilitate the process of enlivenment. Action cues that help 'populate' the drama are usually there for the asking; for example, if a person is mentioned by name, he or she can almost always be included in the action as a real presence. Directors themselves, however, can and do add new elements, according to their sense of the theme of the dialogue (and, inevitably, whatever material of their own they are churning through at the time). For example, if the protagonist says 'I don't want to do this, but I feel I have to', the issue might be taken as one of *guilt* or *judgement*. Instead of setting up 'judgement', which would tend to make the drama one of moral 'types', and therefore rather flat and abstract, the director can steer the action towards a more interpersonal enactment, and ask:

Who is judging? Where does this happen?
Who else is there? Does anyone help you? Does anyone disagree?

These questions are more open than the method in Miro's case. Yet the mode is less cerebral than dealing with abstract qualities; it is more cybernetically faithful, too, provided that director and member do not get together in a 'blaming' posture which might canonize the member's role as victim, and action methods only as redressive.

Let us try again: if a person says that she is 'frightened, self-critical, and impatient', the director can say:

Choose someone who frightens you, someone who is critical of you, someone who is impatient of you.

Or, if they say that they 'don't belong', some relevant questions to generate an interactional sequence might be:

Why not?
Who does belong here?
Where do you belong? Who is there with you?
Who stops them from being with you now?

The expansion from the internal role dialogue to the 'outside' sometimes can occur simply by 'maximizing' the role. In the example below, Minnie is talking to her 'fear'. The director allows her to warm up thoroughly in the inner mode before posing the interpersonal question 'who are you?'.

D: *Are you this far away from Minnie, Fear?*
Fear: *I'm part of her. I come in and out. I operate to disturb her clarity.*

D: *How do you do that?*
Fear: *I go (contemptuously) 'What do you know?', and she (gestures towards Minnie) always answers: 'Nothing'.*
D: *Do it more fully.*
Fear: *What do you know? What do you know?*
D: *Who are you?*
Fear: *I'm her father.*

It is well not to get too carried away with this sort of thing. Although Minnie's director has been more circumspect than Miro's, there are still some hard questions to ask. They would not be asked at this stage, however; to do so would cut across Minnie's warm-up to her 'first story'. Maybe they would be involved in her 'second story'. The issue will hinge around whether Minnie is construing fear as her father as part of her old solution, or whether it is a brand new solution which has a chance of making her happy. Has she learnt to talk this way because she has been around groups for a while? Is therapy in danger of canonizing the actual restraints which it is meant to lift? The answer will most likely come out in the aesthetics of the drama itself. If it looks stale, and the group is bored, chances are that Minnie nominating Fear as her father is not going to do her much good, and will only serve to entrench a quasi-therapeutic language and predictable responses.

Some psychodramatists are most keen to trace the origin of the roles that people take up in internal dialogue to persons from the protagonist's original social atom. Sometimes it indeed seems as if this can be done: after all, they had to have their origin somewhere. But it is easy to fall into a blaming and naive historicism: a cybernetic approach implies that both consultant and client create the text for this story, while simultaneously discovering its meaning (Arcaya, 1985). Together, they progressively elaborate the protagonist's lived experience, and produce a new text. Even this one, of course, is only another 'as if' text, but one hopes it is a wider and wiser story than that experienced by the protagonist before.

The self

From Freud onwards, psychotherapy has been based on the 'realness' of personality – the belief in some essential structure that was the irreducible core of human experience. This belief involved the intellectual creation of various complexes, developmental stages, inevitable dynamics, and 'layers' of consciousness. For Moreno, on the other hand, whose system of thinking was not nearly so scholarly or intricate, roles 'are created before our eyes' (*Psychodrama*, 1972, p. 340). The self-ness of a person is actually an edifice, an impermanent construction that is ever built up and changing on the basis of information from the environment and relationship with others.

If you take it seriously, which few do, Morenian role theory is even today quite radical. Mostly, we think of our 'self' as pretty much bounded by physical parameters. 'We have got used to localizing the conscious personality inside a person's head. I should say an inch or two behind the eyes . . . it is very difficult for us to take stock of the fact that the localization of the personality . . . inside the body is only symbolic, just an aid for practical use' (Wilber, 1977, p. 187).

The notion of roles, however, challenges the assumption that the skin is the most meaningful boundary to an organism. Role theory suggests that we are the creators not only of our experience, but almost of our existence itself. We do not make it up out of nothing, of course, but the storying of our experience, including the notion of 'I' itself, is a collaborative effort between us and others in our social atom. We already understand, if only from our own experience, that people change markedly in different contexts. For example, Tim acts like a pleading, helpless child when he is getting help from a computer expert, but is a kind, firm, and wise figure when he is working as a psychiatric nurse. Similarly, Trudy may behave like a six-year-old when her mum comes to visit, but is a tough union organizer at work. In each of these examples we can see that Tim and Trudy are almost constituted by interaction and context, and by what they tell themselves about themselves, and by what others say their story is. Popular expressions, like 'She was a different person when she came back from holiday', or 'He's a different man with his children' express this sentiment.

Action methods involve far more than the expression of repressed or blocked feelings or an uninhibited cathartic purge (Blatner, 1985). The function of catharsis is not merely emotional relief, but the learning of new roles. The first moment occurs when the emotional truths operating in one's social system become evident with full impact – a person is angry but is not able to experience that feeling because of certain forbidden agendas, say. Expression of the angry feelings via enactment can then be very helpful. Here, action brings up the new, and the result is helpful: at the height of action, the person is in a state of shock – their accustomed responses to a situation are diminished, and new, more primary responses take their place.

Andrew, the alcoholic's son, is stoical and cut-off in a scene when his father is unable to carve the roast at the family dinner. He becomes furious with the father, leaps on him, and tries to shake him 'awake', saying over and over 'Wake up, wake up, wake up, wake up'.

What does Andrew learn, and how does he learn it? According to Morenian theory, Andrew learns a new role or a new set of roles (see also the chapter on 'Warming up'). His actions, feelings, and beliefs towards his alcoholic father have changed from stoic repression, cut off both from the father and the self, to murderous rage; from denial to demand. We might say that the old role was 'Catatonic Repressor', and that the new one is 'Angry Demander'. Andrew's responses of being angry demander and physical opponent have produced changes in the father's role too. When Andrew role reverses with his father, the father also becomes a fighter, rather than a passive alcoholic being shaken by his demanding child. The result of the two of them fighting so wholeheartedly and physically breaks the locked-in, turgid, and intellectualized 'solutions' that have been hitherto tried in the family, and places each person (Andrew and his 'introjected' father) in a new state – that of spontaneity. Now that Andrew's interactions are different, he is, you might say, a 'new person'. His skin is not the only way to define him – there are other boundaries that are also relevant.

Maturana and Varela (1980) and their followers maintain that an organism is as much dependent on connections with the external environment as it is on connections with internal organs such as the heart. A self does not exist solely within the boundary of the skin but extends and connects with the milieux in which it exists. Though an organism is separate and discrete at the level of physical description, it is not separate at other levels of description. At these other levels it defines its form through interaction with others and the environment. The self spreads out beyond the physical boundaries of the person – for example, tribal aboriginals seem strongly to have such a notion of themselves being part of the landscape: the landscape is included in their definition of themselves.

Identity is interactive, a story we tell ourselves and get told. We are shaped, limited, and defined by ideas and restraints. Our limits and boundaries arising from mental distinctions become more or less permanent ideas; they 'catch' and transform the world that comes to us in the form of information. One's 'reality' is the outcome of this information and the way in which it is processed. This matters to consultants: it suggests that if they find a way to change the relevant information flow, the self's construction of reality, including the reality of itself, will alter. If one can enter the system meaning becomes more open to negotiation. When the forbidden agendas are lifted, and a person or group's current story about itself is altered by the assimilation of new information, then this self and the world it construes are changed.

If we 'make ourselves up', then, it would seem a simple matter to change a 'thing' that is so evanescent, so dependent on context and environment. Far from it. We always commence our construction of reality from a previous set of 'givens' – we are not at the mercy of any wind that might blow. We establish a relationship between past and present experiences and thereby create the construct of an inner centre ('me') that is reasonably stable through time. We also gain a sense of the permanence of 'me' and 'my story' because our beliefs about 'what is real' are shaped by our previous constructions of reality. The 'part-ness' of us with everything else means that problems are usually interpersonal, and so is their 'cause'. The conditions of individuation of one person in a group are the conditions of individuation of the others, though the 'evolution' may not always be positive. Change implies different interactions with people, and therefore different roles.

Although complete autonomy is an illusion, one can be relatively autonomous. When we are 'stuck', our stories and prescriptions have worn such deep grooves that observation is only possible to the front, as it were; the 'sides' are too high to see over. We have learnt certain skills and styles all too well, and cannot respond to, or even perceive, new developments as new. But when some of the restraints on being different are lifted, our capacity for exercising influence in the system (spontaneity) is increased. Spontaneity is present to the extent that someone can rise above and change the way they act in a system. Quite on their own they can leap out of a rutted path into a new, less worn one. It is a miracle. As you saw in the preceding chapter, when people cannot perform the miracle alone, they get the outsider in.

Chapter four

Focusing the conflict

But you know very well, Miss Loy, that here in England love and hate are two entirely different things. They are not even opposites. According to my outlook, love comes in the first place from the heart and hate rises basically from principle.

Muriel Spark

By now you may agree that the process of drama almost always includes externalization – setting an 'object' outside the self and interacting with it. Drama requires at least two of you: you and a 'part' of yourself; you and another person; or even you and a decision you have to make. Therefore even the simplest exercise contains some form of dialectic:

Use two chairs to represent what you give to the group and what you get from the group; place them as wide apart or as close as you like.

By a stroke of luck, perhaps, externalization can fit neatly into a systems framework: the very process of externalization (usually called 'concretization' in the psychodramatic literature) automatically creates a 'double description' of self and not-self. Members see the difference, act it, become both sides of it. On stage, the thrilling winds of change may blow as strongly as they do because double description is actually built in to the process.

This chapter moves from the self/other dialectic that you have just been reading about into a 'focal conflict' model of understanding problems and working with groups. The model was originally devised by French (1952, 1954) essentially for analytic work, but it successfully catches the many-sidedness of reality. It has been adapted by Whitaker and Lieberman (1964), by Whitaker (1982, 1985) herself, and more lately by psychodramatist Max Clayton to link group-level and individual dynamics. As you read through the chapter, you may begin to see that a dialectical structure is yet another way of attaining double description. Some training exercises in dialectical methods are given in the next chapter, where you will have the best chance of practising from the model. The model is picked up again later in the book in the chapter on 'Failure in warm-up'.

Focal conflict

Reader, I am sure that you do not need reminding that you cannot have everything in this life – that lesson, alas, is daily brought home. Various writers, not least Karl Marx, have placed an intellectual framework around the dialectic of desires and the set-backs to them at the personal, economic, and cultural levels. In the psychological field, however, which is the one of most relevance to this discussion, dialectical frameworks have not exactly been headline news. Let me at least push them a little here, because they are once again a way of habituating one's theoretical processes to double description.

According to French, 'nuclear conflicts' become established in the family of origin, and remain in adult life. They consist of a core wish or impulse (the 'disturbing motive') – for example, the wish for nurturance, which is in conflict with a 'reactive motive' (for example, a pervasive feeling of being unlovable). As a way of dealing with this conflict, a person adopts one or several 'solutions' which serve to contain the fears but nevertheless allow for some satisfaction of the wish; for example, by taking the role of 'Stubborn Loner' (solution), one can deny (reactive motive) the need (disturbing motive) for close relationships. While the *solution* remains in force in adult life, says French, the disturbing and reactive motives rarely last in consciousness; the fears and wishes sink away, leaving just the habit or typical interaction (solution). A solution, in effect, is anything we actually do. In adult life, maintains Whitaker (1985), not so much nuclear conflicts as *focal* conflicts emerge which are similar to the original nuclear conflict. A person experiences wishes and fears which are basically the same as those involved in the nuclear conflict, but which are infused with the *present situation*.

To return to the group context: in response to these wishes and fears a group member is likely to invoke habitual solutions, not always well adapted to the demands of the present. This is where action methods have a place: for example, the idea of 'disturbing motives' can easily be expanded to include the hunger for psychodramatic roles. These are the universal human urges for perfectibility – the forces which drive people on and make them want to transcend their present state. Examples of such drives are the desire for adventure; the desire to enrich oneself by learning; the desire for immortality; the desire to be god; the desire to reach out to one's fellow human beings; the desire to protect the planet; and so on. The following quotation from Moreno is a fine example of presenting a disturbing motive, in this case the idealized vision of children's complete spontaneity. Moreno's writing, like most inspirational texts, reflects this side of a dialectic:

When I look at a child, I see 'Yes, yes, yes, yes'. They do not have to

> learn to say 'No'. Being born is yes. You see spontaneity in the living form. It is written all over the child, in his act hunger, as he looks at things, as he listens to things, as he rushes into time, as he moves into space, as he grabs for objects, as he smiles and cries.
>
> (Moreno, in Fox (1987, p. 206))

To reiterate: if the disturbing motive is a radical force which leads people 'out' towards adventure, learning, curiosity, or love, the *reactive motive* is what tends to prevent these desires from being enacted. The reactive motive contains the forbidden agendas, the restraints on change. It is a conservative force that pulls people back 'in' towards stasis. The reactive motive also usually involves 'reality' elements and negative self-talk, such as despair, criticism, and fear: fear of betrayal; fear of hurting ourselves, of hurting someone else, of being lonely, of being poor, rejected, and so on. Forbidden agendas are constituted by these restraints on change, some of which may be conscious – one might actually know most of one's fears, for example – but most of which operate outside consciousness.

The *solution* is what we actually do to resolve the dialectic. It is important to note that the solution is by no means always the ideal solution; it is simply the solution adopted at the time. In our lives very often the solution is to keep the voice of the disturbing motive down, and go along with the voice of the reactive motive. That is, 'stay put' may become a solution, and is of course sometimes an entirely sensible one. In Whitaker's terms, solutions are rarely perfect or ideal, but are more or less 'enabling' or 'restrictive'. Restrictive solutions keep us as stuck as we are, or make us even more stuck. Enabling solutions allow us to approach the ideal a little more closely, even though we may never meet it. As none of us can ever live out fully our disturbing motives, the point of consultation is to give more scope for relatively enabling solutions while not canonizing restrictive solutions.

In any endeavour, the hero (now a unisex word) is not a person who struggles once, gloriously, and wins. Rather, success implies a return to the struggle again and again until victory is won. Nevertheless, heroes tend to choose enabling rather than restrictive types of solutions to dilemmas, even if the particular solution chosen does not work out. They try a new one. Any 'victory' of course, is merely the start of a new cycle of disturbing motives, reactive motives, and solutions. Few of us win all the time, few of us manage to live out our dream to the fullest. The psychodramatic 'solution' is nevertheless to engage more fully in the process of life, to keep favouring the disturbing motive – one never 'wins' at life, anyway. The way a director helps a group towards such solutions is by unravelling the forbidden agendas lurking in the reactive motive.

The focal conflict model has been presented to you at some length because it is as syntonic with the strategic frame as it is with a cybernetic and action understanding of the world. Strategic action consultants focus on people's solutions, enquiring how the solution itself helps to maintain the problem. In fact, the solution is often presented *as* the problem or symptom. The complaint, however unwanted, can be understood in terms of the function that it is fulfilling for the person or their system. That function (for example, 'to stay a depressed bachelor in order to stop mother feeling bad about herself') may have long since ceased (after all, mother is dead) but the story or narrative around the events may persist.

Our solutions are not all 'bad', of course: we have to do *something*. But a model with double description built into it has the advantage of being able to focus on the strengths as well as the difficulties a person has. Enabling solutions allow some gratification of the disturbing motive and are functional for relationships with others; but restrictive solutions operate to a person's disadvantage, and to the disadvantage of other people, and make it difficult for them to attain the peace and joys they seek. Because a reactive motive – let us say, of fear – is operating when the situation does not actually call for it, people meet events with inappropriate solutions. They lose spontaneity, and repeat behaviours in a 'stuck' fashion. They are responding not to the situation, but to some forbidden agenda which does not allow them to reconstrue the situation in a fresh way.

Solutions, even dysfunctional ones, are sometimes labelled as 'defences'. This sort of language is probably less helpful than to think of them as ways of acting that make the best sense to people, even if they do not turn out very well. Nor need they be construed solely in terms of individual dynamics – one adopts a particular solution not just to help oneself, but also to help someone else, even if this 'help' may be misguided, and does not really help the other person at all. That is, from the example above, now-deceased mother is certainly not helped in her own feelings about sexual worthiness by son remaining a depressed bachelor, and nor was she when she was alive. The son's help, though touchingly loyal, is dysfunctional for him and for her.

Forbidden agendas do not usually concern the self only, but others in the social atom: perhaps the agenda is to maintain an alliance or coalition with someone in the family, or to prevent an alliance or coalition breaking up. For instance, a daughter may become very depressed as a way of taking her parents' minds off their own sorrows: if they worry about her, they cannot worry about themselves and become even more depressed, she (unconsciously) reasons. A young boy may indulge in a stint of car theft just as his mother is going back to study, because he believes (not consciously, of course) that something bad will happen to his dad or to the family if she becomes too competent.

Such 'solutions' may be transitory or permanent – that is, one may employ them only for a particular context, or in particular interactions. But to construe them exclusively in terms of 'loss of love' or 'fear of abandonment' for *oneself* (that is, to work exclusively in an individual rather than an interpersonal or systemic frame) would often be to miss the point. It would also be missing the point to construe them as 'defensive' – as often as not they are altruistic, even though the altruism may not actually help anybody. We more often do things *for* someone, rather than against them, even if the doing wrecks our own lives and in fact does not do much for dear old dad. This is all out of consciousness, of course. When one is consulting to a group, the relevant alliances and coalitions may well be in the group itself, especially if it has been meeting for some time (see 'Strategic sociometry').

Using the focal conflict model: the boyfriend

Let us see how this framework of disturbing motive, reactive motive, and solution would work out in action in a group setting. Marina has said in the group that she wants to work on her relationship with her boyfriend, Boyd, 'who's just a user', but that she does not want to do it 'just now'. After an extended conversation with Marina in which she asked the usual strategic questions ('How is this problem a problem?'; 'How long has this problem been around?', etc.), Dot conceptualizes to herself Marina's difficulties in this way:

She wants to change her relationship with her boyfriend – disturbing motive.
She is afraid that something bad will happen to her or to him if she does so – reactive motive.
She wants to put off dealing with this matter until later; her solution is so-called 'procrastination', perhaps . . . this is borne out by her body language. 'Maybe', thinks Dot, 'she deals with her anger by procrastinating, because the effect she's having in the group is to make people feel baffled and ashamed, but they're blocked from saying anything because she seems so helpless and vague. But I wonder if she is restrained from liveliness and spontaneity by trying to help or show loyalty (forbidden agenda) to anyone here. Mmmm . . . I think I'll try the easy bit first.'

Dot's next step is to put some of this structure to Marina in the group, being careful to pose it in a way that will be helpful to her. If she takes away Marina's habitual solution too quickly, she will leave her in a position where her underlying fears are no longer being contained. If that does happen, she must help make the group a safe environment where the fears can be confronted. It is a delicate balance: to produce enough warm-up so that the dilemma is alive, and at the same time give Marina the opportunity to confront her fears and test whether, whatever their origin, they need to apply here. Marina may have adopted her solution a long time ago, when it was functional or necessary for her to act this way. It may not be so now, however, since she has gained adulthood and with it more experience and strength. The forbidden agendas, if exposed with delicacy, may lose their potency. So Dot says to Marina and the group:

Let's stop and think for a moment. You're all here for a serious purpose. For example, you, Marina, want to complete something, but something is stopping you. You want to have a relationship that is full and rich, eh – one where you'll feel free to develop yourself?

Dot's statement of the disturbing motive is posed in terms of deep inner needs. She couches her language in terms specific to Marina's own statements, and also in universal human desires: 'complete something'; 'full and rich'; 'feel free'; 'develop yourself'. By thus semi-hypnotically tapping in to wishes that will catch just about anyone, Dot gives something for the group to relate to, so that they warm up with Marina. What Marina wants is not something that, even if the conflict is resolved, will necessarily be given in its entirety. Yet the *desire* for it may be the very source of the conflict.

Dot makes it her practice to explore thoroughly the reactive motive in dialectical relationship to the ideals that have been expressed. Paradoxically, by full expression of the reactive motive, the action that has been suppressed in life starts to be expressed in the group. The 'relative influence' of the disturbing and reactive motives can then be assessed and used by each person. 'How much influence does the disturbing motive have, how much the reactive, and which side is winning?' are questions in Dot's mind, and ones that she may on occasion directly pose to an individual or to the whole group.

This is why a restraints-based interview is couched in dialectic form rather than in the form of exhortation to improve. After all, the group members have probably been doing this to themselves for most of their lives; it is also part of their own restrictive solutions overtly to resist such exhortations, or perhaps to become penitent or self-conscious. In either instance, the solution stays the same. By heightening the yes/no struggle, the director attempts to have people contact that inner 'Yes', which often seems like madness. The inner 'Yes' frequently has the impulses or the visions that we hide as being too psychotic to reveal to others. It is often more clearly revealed by exposing what is blocking it – the 'No'. By exposing the 'No', the director is beginning, paradoxically, the process of what Yalom (1975) calls 'the instillation of hope'.

Maybe there's a fear that you will not have enough time to do it now. Maybe you feel that if you do it here, you'll be committed to something that you'll regret, eh? (Dot can keep on giving reasons in the reactive motive, if it seems appropriate.)

Many of us prefer to say 'No' rather than 'Yes' to chance opportunities that present themselves. Those who say 'Yes', as Keith Johnstone (1979) remarks, are usually rewarded by the excitement of their life, while those who say 'No' are rewarded by the safety of their lives. (Actually, of course, we need both No and Yes, stability and change. Not all change is good, and not all stability is bad.) Compliant people tend to favour the reactive motive to the adventures that suggest themselves throughout the day, and during most interactions with others. They not only have their own talent eroded, but by applying restrictive solutions to others, they limit other people's lives, too. People with dull lives appear to think that their lives are dull by chance; but in fact we have some choice over whether our lives are dull or not through our patterns of blocking or yielding, saying 'No' or saying 'Yes'. Action methods heighten this dialectic, especially when a restraints-based interview is conducted. Dot has been attempting to develop, to maximize and highlight some of the points at which participants say 'No'. This is not perverse, tricky, or eccentric of her; she does it for reasons that may now be coming clear.

You may find that a group functions best when the reactive motive is worked with and recognized. If the disturbing motive is developed exclusively (a pep talk), the person's restrictive solution, which is a 'defence' against the disturbing motive, can easily become part of the norm of the group. Only after careful development of the reactive motive can the exceptions to the dysfunctional solutions safely be raised. In her processes, Dot tries to assess how much emphasis there is in the group on expression and how much emphasis there is on holding on.

(To Marina) There are varying solutions to this conflict, I suppose; for example, you can wait and go to another group at some future time to work on this. Or you can wait until tomorrow. Or you can see what Boyd himself throws up. Which do you think is more in charge at the moment – the desire to get somewhere with Boyd, or the fear that something dreadful will happen if you do?

Dot here builds up the relative influence questioning on the dilemma and remains neutral on the solution. She aims to arouse Marina and the group to creative aspects of themselves. From here she can use action around either the solution or the disturbing or reactive motives. For example, she might choose to work with the simplest forms of action methods, and say:

You, Marina, have decided on a wait-and-see policy. Use this chair out here and have a consultation with the Marina who waits and sees.

But she can also leave Marina for the moment and throw the action open to the group to gain a greater group warm-up. The group needs to be kept near the edge of action, or the possibility of action. If Dot spends too long in a counselling-type relationship with Marina, forming an exclusive twosome with her, the group may become warmed up to their own feelings of jealousy or exclusion. This sort of warm-up, of course, is quite opposite to the one intended.

Marina says that she wants to wait and see. What do you respond to that, Mabel?. . . . What is going on in you as you witness this, Monty?

Dot says something to a few people so that group involvement goes on. She does it lightly and quickly, not making interventions at this stage that will stop the group:

A number of people are focused on relationships – they are not getting what they want out of them. You want fuller relationships, but something, perhaps some fear, is pulling you back. Maybe you're adopting the solution of holding still and just despairing. Where do you put yourself in relation to Marina on this, Mort?

Her last question to Mort, of course, has been a 'sociometric' one (see later chapters) in which Marina's solution becomes a criterion against which the group can measure themselves. This is another way of getting into action, but it will not be developed until Part II of this book.

Dot tries to maintain the affective level, tuning in to non-verbal responses, as well as what people actually say: 'I see you're interested in this, Maurice. You're nodding as you watch. There's something stirring inside you (disturbing motive again). And you're probably responding to the fear that's in this room as well (reactive motive). What do you do when you sense fear? (enquiry about solution).' She binds in several group members to the interaction, which by now may not be about Marina at all, but about Monty. The process can be repeated over and over until a suitable customer is found, or the session ends.

Chapter five

Responding to the problem

You *can* have your cake and eat it; the only trouble is you get fat.

Julian Barnes

Group members often talk of their difficulties in terms of 'terminal hypotheses' – descriptions of themselves that have no implications for change. A person may say: 'I can't love anyone', or 'I'm just a scared person, I suppose', or 'I just don't seem to have the will-power to stop eating'. Ultimately, the director wants to offer a new description that will outlast the old one. The first step is to reframe the complaint dialectically so that it is no longer expressed as a terminal hypothesis, but already has the notion of change written into it. Dialectical representation of the complaint, as you may have noticed in the previous chapter, takes the form of: 'You want to . . . (disturbing motive), but . . . (reactive motive) is stopping you at the moment; and so you . . . (solution).' The dialectical format can be used when talking to an individual or to the group at large. In the latter instance the 'solution' refers to some solution adopted by the whole group, for example to fight with each other or with the leader.

Once again, I am perhaps making all this sound a little too easy, maybe giving the impression that you would offer a focal conflict description all at once, and irrespective of timing. Sadly, this would not work at all. It does take a measure of skill to deliver a focal intervention, in terms of its timing and phrasing, etc.; but delivery, in a sense, is the easy part. The hard part is even to think in dialectical terms, and especially to pick out the relevant disturbing motive, which is often sunk deep in the forbidden agendas of the person or group.

Dialectical thinking is the hard part . . . and since this chapter is essentially a training chapter, an immediate start could be made with some training. After a short time you may get a 'feel' for this sort of work, and decide whether it suits your sort of person or not. Begin with some forms of the dialectic that might apply to you personally, and then move to more general forms – ones that do not require application to a specific person or situation, but might fit most human beings.

(a) Make a list of your own disturbing motives – those urges that inspire you to take positive action, whether or not you do so.
(b) Make a list of 'universal' disturbing motives, such as might apply to almost anybody.
(c) Make a list of your own reactive motives.
(d) Make a list of 'universal' reactive motives such as might apply to almost anybody.

Dialectical descriptions, such as the ones you have just been practising, are not limited by what members are attempting to do for themselves. Such a focus ignores the social definitions of what a 'self' is that have been explored in the last two chapters. A self is only relatively autonomous; and a self is far from self-ish. It is a safe bet to say that people act not only to enhance themselves, but out of 'invisible loyalties' to others, whether living or dead. Indeed, some of our 'worst' actions are performed out of love or loyalty, no matter how misguided or unnecessary that love or loyalty may now be.

So group members (and all of us, for that matter) may act as if they are still responding to their family-of-origin, rather than to people actually present in the group. In treating other group members as people from their own family, participants may appear to be protecting someone, distracting someone, admonishing someone, or attempting to keep the whole group stable by taking on a particular form of behaviour. Even at their most hostile, they may be being true to a memory, or protecting someone in the here and now. Often that 'someone' is not themselves, though it certainly seems so at times – one cannot be too absolute about this. But in any case, these forms of behaviour may seem very odd until understood systemically; people tend to operate simultaneously within two systems – a 'virtual' system from their original social atom, and the system that is constituted in the actual here-and-now; that is, the social atom of the group.

Working on the present, working on the problem

I have suggested several times that there is no 'really real' to get back to. One description of what is 'real' is supplanted by another, and not only in therapy. So regardless of the basic aetiology of difficulties that people bring to a group, they persist only if they are maintained by the ongoing behaviour of those with whom they interact. If there is no freezer, the ice will melt.

That is why the *present* is often a good locus for consultation, and why groupwork is sometimes unjustly despised amongst strategic therapists. Now, there is nothing against forays into the past, as you know, if a good double description can be concocted there. But if the present problem-maintaining behaviour (that is, the stance that other members take up towards the person, and their attempted solutions) is shifted, the problem itself may vanish. Who knows? Despite a therapist's best efforts, the *origins* of a problem – the invisible loyalties to people in the past – may never be fully understood. But how those invisible loyalties are enacted to people in the present is a crucial focus for work in the group. You may find too that they usually emerge as secret alliances and are often the most forbidden of the forbidden agendas, the secret of secrets.

Strategic consultants like to define what the job is, and to get out when it is done; from the very start they set up with the client a time when they will not be needed any more. They are rather practical, sleeves-rolled-up sorts of people who become unhappy when a group does not seem to be working on a problem. Now, some people think that it is shallow and in poor taste to work on a problem in therapy – rather like mentioning money in a good club. They believe that therapy should work on wisdom and enlightenment, and perhaps they are right. The question of whether one can or should speak of 'a problem' as if it were something existing on its own will continually haunt this narrative. Is group consultancy a matter of pragmatics and problem solving, or does it involve aesthetics, enlightenment, and epiphany?. . . . Ah, you have probably guessed the answer already.

It is not particularly a long-term method; in fact strategic workers tend to be concerned about long bouts of therapy. They do not subscribe to the view that all change is necessarily slow and measured – on the contrary, rapid, all-or-nothing change is also common in nature and in human affairs, especially in a period of crisis. So in their opinion, change may take a while or it may be quick. Similarly, they take an unusual stance on the 'past', so often the rich field of long-term therapy: while acknowledging that historically generated family constructs may well be the source of the forbidden agendas, they prefer to work with current interactions. Mind you, they will work anywhere they see some leverage, so it is not that they do not 'believe' in the past, or in its power over the present. For example, they may hypothesize at the level of the past about why the present may be as it is, but direct most of their energies to altering current interactions. They figure that altering current response patterns can be as effective as a deep understanding of the origins of those patterns. Their experience tells them that even a slight alteration in the social atom, if timed well, can reverberate into the future in a most astonishingly powerful way.

Empathy?

By now you have probably realized that expressing yourself in terms of focal conflicts requires a deep 'reaching in' to the other person's processes. In short, it is like the well-known therapeutic skill of empathy.

A word of caution is in order here, though. While the ability to empathize with others' experience is fundamental to any group leader, the director may nevertheless decide not to use this skill extensively with an individual group member beyond the process of basic 'joining' with him or her. Sometimes empathic statements only reflect underlying feelings of hopelessness and self-doubt – in short, the reactive motive, without adequately providing a base in distinction for a person to be able to move.

(a) Form pairs, and each of you discuss three current difficulties, whether major or minor, in your lives. When you have done that for a minute or two, practise framing the affect and content of your partner's discourse in terms of disturbing motives, reactive motives, and the solutions.

(b) Assist your partner with a sculpture of a particular focal conflict in their lives. Exaggerate one of the poles, then the other. Change the solution and then see what happens to either of the poles.

(c) 'Reframe' a particular reactive motive in three different ways, all of them positive. That is, communicate to your partner what they are trying to achieve by the reactive motive.

(d) Tell two anecdotes from your own life which have the embedded structure of disturbing motive, reactive motive, and solution.

(e) Tell these anecdotes to the group at large, as if you were a director beginning a group.

Empathy, and 'joining the system' is certainly required in groups; but it also needs to be of such a kind as can rapidly translate a member's statement dialectically into a double description. For example, suppose that the person says that they are 'seductive'. This appellation can be translated as 'wanting to be liked', or 'wanting to surround yourself with many people who affirm you'. With such a reformulation, the *purpose* (disturbing motive) of a characteristic makes more sense within the person's system. The function of the reformulation is not to ingratiate the director with the participant, but to provide an avenue down which they both might move. The second description can then be introduced: 'But your efforts to do this do not convince you of your likeableness.' The third side of the focal conflict (the current solution) may then be stated: 'Therefore you try over and over again.'

Weeks (1977) has given a list of changes from negative self-labels to positive reformulations. For example, he redefines 'passive' as 'ability to accept things as they are'; 'controlling' as 'structuring one's environment', and 'oppositional' as 'searching for one's own way of doing things'. It is of little use, however, to learn such a list and apply it whenever the trigger words come up, as the context of the statement is highly relevant. We are not so much interested in 'positive reformulations' as being able to locate a complaint in terms of double description. I am arguing for the type of reformulation that is elaborated fully in a dialectical mode.

Give three different reformulations to each of the following statements, imagining a different context for each statement – 'I am depressed'; 'I am stuck'; 'I'm a really shy person'. Shape them out more fully into a focal conflict involving disturbing motive, reactive motive, and solution.

Participants often interpret their own behaviour, or that of others, in ways that make for continuing difficulties. When the meaning attributed to the behaviour is redefined, even this simple action can have a powerful effect on how the member makes sense of things. The member offers one construct of reality; the leader offers another which goes deep into the person's meaning world. The redefinition suggested by the leader may not, in fact, be any more or less 'true' than the original definition of the problem offered by the participant. But some labels provoke difficulties, while others promote new ways of learning.

The relative influence of the problem

Does your theory have more influence on you than you have on your theory? This type of question does not at first seem to make sense. But if you attempt to answer it for yourself, you may find you have to go deep into your own epistemology. Probing the relative influence of X (say, alcohol usage) over someone versus the influence they have over X is a typical process of strategic work, and has been refined by family therapists such as Penn (1982), Tomm (1987), and especially White (1986, 1988, 1989) and White and Epston (1989). The question of the influence of your theory over you versus the influence of you over your theory, by the way, is an interesting one to attempt to answer for itself, and also for the way it is put. As you are by now aware, it 'externalizes' theory from yourself in a most unusual way.

The process might even be said to be a little shocking, especially to those who may have been brought up in the Gestalt tradition of 'owning' and 'taking responsibility'. Well, rest assured – the procedure of locating responsibility in the interpersonal system is not intended to make people more feckless, immature, and irresponsible. Externalization of the problem is entirely in the service of creating new descriptions that outlast the old descriptions, and is a special case of dialectical reformulation. Indeed, when problems are externalized, the group has already participated in a new description of them – an externalized description. 'Relative influence questioning' (see White, 1988) invites members to derive two different descriptions of their problem. The first is a description of the influence of the problem on their lives, and the second is a description of the influence of the life over the problem. Even if the problem has apparently saturated their life, there are areas where it does not. Members have to account in some way for the contradictions involved in being problem-soaked.

Relative influence work is highly relevant to strategic methods. It is more complex than simply externalizing the problem and having the person struggle with it (though that is often a helpful enough procedure in itself, mind you). It almost consists of marshalling two armies – those that are for the problem, and those that are against it within the person. A simple form of relative influence externalization can be to ask the person working on the problem what 'starves' and what 'feeds' the problem – this gives the problem a life of its own, external from the person. A stepwise form would look like this:

1. *Warm the person up to the problem.*

2. *Isolate the problem, and choose an auxiliary to be it.*

3. *Ask the person whether at the moment the problem is 'in control' or whether they are in control. Ask whether the problem has established a 'trend' (White, 1986) in recent times, and how long the trend has been trending. If appropriate, enact a scene when the problem first began to be a problem. Enact a scene in the present, and comment on the difference between the original scene and this one.*

4. *Ask the person what behaviours of their own and factors in their life 'starve' the problem, and choose auxiliaries for each of these.*

5. *Ask the person what behaviours of their own and factors in their life 'feed' the problem, and choose auxiliaries for each of these.*

6. *Have the whole system thus created interact, with person role reversing into each part.*

7. *(and most important) Follow up in successive weeks about which 'side' is winning.*

Although this formula may look simple, it can be most powerful. On one side, the problem's power is mapped, and on the other the person's power, even if it is small, is also mapped (White, 1989). Directors assist members to identify the problem's sphere of influence, facilitating a full problem-saturated description of life in the social atom. The influence of the problem is not contained in the single group member, but is between him or her and various persons and various relationships. Once a description of the problem's sphere of influence has been derived, a second enactment and description can take place: the influence of the group member on the life of the problem. Ordinarily, members will have difficulty with this second type of description, and they need encouragement.

That they can do so at all seems to come from the externalization itself – somehow having one's problem (alcoholism, bed-wetting, marital difficulties, etc.) 'outside' oneself seems to give one a handle on it. The very charting of the influence of 'it' versus you makes the it somehow more manageable. Externalization seems to break the mesmeric hold that the problem has on the person; people are freer in their perception of events surrounding the problem and the way it had got a stranglehold on relationships. In the old 'map', the problem's sphere of influence, like the red of the British Empire, may have seemed to cover the globe. When the map is redrawn, little bits of the person's own colours start to leak over; tiny revolutions and independence movements seem to be having success. The person's life is no longer so 'colonized' by the problem.

The process would not be successful if the influence of the problem were not fully drawn, so that the influence of the person appears in relief. Not only should people not be cut off in their problem description, but it can form the major part of any consultancy. Then either the person him or herself (spontaneously) or the director (artfully) begins to contradict the problem-saturated description. For the life of me, Reader, I cannot explain more fully why this is so; relative influence questioning and enactments where the problem is externalized seem to be most powerful ways of bringing change. One tends to doubt it, not because the process is particularly difficult, but for the opposite reason: something as useful as this should not be so simple.

Responding to responses

There is a snag: the effects of this work do not so much come from the heat and light of a dramatic display, but from the externalization itself, and especially from the follow-up. This means that the practice is of almost no use as a one-off as its force comes from the following-through over time; when the initial change is instituted, the gap has to be widened by 'responding to responses'. 'Widening the gap' needs to be a regular process until the change is well in place. No check-out on change usually equals no change.

Responding to responses (White, 1986), therefore, forms possibly the most important part of any consultancy. It is a way of capitalizing on and expanding any change by bringing news of difference to it. To start with, the director begins enquiries, a week or more after the drama, on what the changes have been, positive or negative. This procedure might at first appear risky or naive to you. It might even seem rather impertinent, like begging the question or asking for praise. The intention is far from that, and if you are in the appropriate role, you will not get much by way of praise anyway. It is a professional and technical procedure with little room for a swelled head. You can pat yourself on the back after they have all gone home, if the responding to responses has been successful.

In assuming change after a session, you are actually on safe ground, even though the inquiry may initially be met with a denial of any difference. Changes will have occurred, but not have been noticed; it is a cybernetic axiom that an unnoticed change has less chance of survival than a noticed change. It does not even matter whether the action has been particularly vivid or grand, or whether the change has come from the session or not – *something* will be different in a week or a fortnight, and it is on that that you capitalize. The differences sought are preferably in behaviour, but differences in thinking or feeling will suffice. Usually these will in any case have led to one small change in the person's outer life, and this can be used as a shoehorn for further changes.

Responding to responses is best done not just once, but several times:

Mindy, what's different now?. . . . Have there been occasions in the last few weeks when you were nearly overwhelmed by those difficulties you worked on in the drama, but somehow managed to undermine them? What was the time you most felt like quitting? When was a time you thought you'd got a handle on this thing at last?

As I have said, the director asks not just for feeling states that have changed – though these are very important – but the bonus is getting Mindy to notice different things she is doing, and then to ask what new feelings or thoughts accompany the new ways of acting. Either way round will do. In the extract below, the director's job is very easy. She only has to keep M going noticing the differences. M draws from all parts of human experience – her inner world and her outer world of relationships – even finance makes an appearance.

The woman who nearly died

Merle is a 32-year-old graduate student who participated in a weekend course in psychodrama. A year previously she had nearly died of leukaemia, and at the course was still showing many of the physical effects, especially fatigue, susceptibility to common illnesses, and extreme weight loss. During the weekend she had done a very short action sequence (about five minutes) where she became a karate expert taking on death.

At the time of reporting, she is still on a post-workshop 'high' three weeks later (somewhat understandably, as you will see). Her direct involvement in the weekend had been so brief that Danny almost neglected to question her on any changes. Fortunately, he did remember, for this is what she said:

M: I felt so whole. Everything I was thinking and feeling I was saying to the people around me. People responded with a lot of intimacy. I can let go of things much more now.

D: How astonishing! Anything else?

M: (crying) Yes, when I got back my little boy yelled at me. He'd been so perfect for eighteen months, trying not to upset mummy and make her die.

D: Goodness! How have you managed all this? Any other changes that you can think of?

M: No, I don't think so. . . . I don't think you'd really count the. . . . Oh, and my husband has changed – he's not so horribly supportive. He'd been financially supportive too, all through my illness. He was trying to be beside my bed every day in the hospital, and be the big provider at the same time. I'd no idea the strain that put him under. He got drunk last Saturday.

D: (a little overwhelmed) Well, perhaps that's enough. Could we now. . . .

M: (conversationally) On Sunday we put the house on the market. We're moving downmarket, and I'm as pleased as punch. My being ill for so long, and Harry visiting me all the time, and living in this huge bloody pile . . . it's a nice house, actually, but we're sick of the strain. We're going to live in a cheaper house and just relax for a while. Does that count? (She goes on in this vein for some time, and at this and other times – not reported here – makes repeated gestures of thanks and praise for Danny's abilities.)

D: (recovering) Well, actually, I'm a bit worried by the speed of these changes. There'll come a time when you may want to go back to how things were. How do you think you'll manage those times? What resources do you and your family have to draw on?

Although he is nearly as delighted as Merle herself, he goes into the 'improvement routine' for the end of a case (see Brennan and Williams (1988) for a fuller description of this process). It is not a matter of scepticism about change or even post-workshop highs that leads him to do this, but a strategic stance taken so that the new outlasts the old. So while he is certainly glad of the changes, it will be of little help to Merle if she attributes them to a 'miracle' session, or if the problem-dissolved descriptions of her life do not outlast the problem-saturated descriptions.

His stance means less pats on the back as he diverts her attention away from the dramatic encounter with himself and into her own life and own resources. Shrugging off the pats on the back should not be a churlish or ungracious process, however, if the protagonist is determined to give them – it is no use getting into a fight if someone wants to thank you. Nor are his deflections merely a matter of charm and modesty – directors are as vain as anyone else in the human race. But in truth, it is not he who 'did' it – it is she, and so he can deflect her praise back on to herself with complete integrity. Responding to responses is as much part of the job as conducting the drama.

The bottomless pit

In the extract below, the director is having some difficulty in getting M, who reports change, to be explicit. He wants her to be explicit, not in the least because he thinks she is lying about the changes, but so that she herself will continue to be affected by the news of difference. It is easier to remember and repeat something you have *done* that is different than it is to remember and repeat an emotional state. As often as not, of course, the emotional state is the motor and the steering wheel to affect change in what one does. Doing, thinking, and feeling are equally important, and change can start with any one of them.

M: (Two weeks after a drama on loss in her social atom from childhood to the present) I've felt much more confident with my quieter side.

D: Quieter, eh? Can you give me a picture of what you mean? What do you do that's different now you're quieter?

M: I'm not expecting as much from people as I have in the past. I'm finding it hard to describe – when I was doing the drama, I could hear the echoes of people in the group crying and sobbing. In all those years, I didn't experience any comfort in all those losses. But I did feel comfort at last a couple of weeks ago.

D: Amazing. How did you let yourself feel that? How come you didn't stop it or discount it?

M: (apparently ignoring him) I had an extraordinary dream on Sunday night. I was walking past the house I grew up in. It was all brightly painted. I looked into the back and there was a new garden with beautiful flowers. I've never had a dream like that about that house – usually it's all dark.

I had a second dream. I am in my bedroom as a girl. An enormous dark figure jumped up. I thought it was a man. It was like the angel of death in that room.

D: What did you make of it? How come these dreams were so different?

M: I dunno. I was . . . calm.

D: How do you account for being calm when you see the angel of death?

M: It's to do with acceptance. I can't explain it.

D: *How have relationships at home been since that weekend?*
M: *(apparently ignoring him again) All my life I've been a bottomless pit of need. I expected people close to me to know my needs without saying. But I told you all I was upset. You saw me.*
D: *(persevering) And at home?*
M: *I'm light. The pit of need was abandonment – feeling desolate and not comforted. At home I'm not stretching out looking for this pit to be filled.*
D: *That's an extraordinary thing! After such a long habit of being a 'pit'. Don't you think the change was a bit quick? Wouldn't you like to go back to your old ways?*
M: *(indignant) No I would not! I'm sick of it. I like me better this way, and everyone else does too.*
D: *Who's most affected by that, do you think?*
M: *Joe, my middle son.*
D: *So what does Joe notice that you do differently?*
(They continue in this vein for some time.)

Where possible, a director notes the replies of former protagonists after the first set of responding to responses, and then asks them again in a further two weeks or so what the changes have been, whether they have kept them up, whether there have been any new changes, who else has noticed, and so on. In other words, the process is repeated. The director may express surprise that Max or Mindy or Mick or Merle has managed to change so much in such a short time, and where appropriate go into 'the improvement routine', suggesting the dangers of changing so quickly, asking whether they did not prefer their old lifestyle, with all its problems, to this new one, and so on. It is quite easy actually to get a change through action methods – the secret is to get the change to stick around.

Part two

Warm-up and sociometry

Chapter six

Warming up

God protect me from the person who makes believe they're not vulgar.

Carl Whitaker

Starters

We quite understandably link our images of 'warm-up' with those of physical movement. An athlete does exercises, takes a massage, and runs a few easy laps of a track before a race; a dancer bends and stretches, shakes, props, and swivels prior to a performance; a team of footballers pass the ball to each other and give bloodcurdling yells before a match. In these models, the warming-up process is physical, prior to the 'main event', and separate from it. The division is not so clear, however, in action methods, where warming up is actually part of the 'main event' of whatever we are doing. It never stops. It is at once prior and present. Moreno (1953, p. 42) called it 'the operational expression of spontaneity'. Warm-up not only leads to and triggers a new state, but continues as new roles emerge: the warm-up and the act become one. You saw some examples of warming up flowing from role to role in Chapter 2.

Here is another example of continuous warm-up, a little closer to home. Your beginning to read this current chapter is, I trust, a warm-up to the roles of 'Curious Learner' or 'Informed Practitioner'; you hope to read of ideas that have not occurred to you, or that confirm what you have known for a long time. But these are just some of your roles likely to be activated; 'Indignant Critic', for example, may come to the fore as you strike something you do not agree with, or the role of 'Opportunistic Professional' may be activated as you come across an exercise that can be used for a group you yourself are running soon.

As you read on, something may cause you to reflect on yourself and your relationship with others. You rise to personal issues involving a puzzle facing you at the moment, and for a while enter the role of 'Life Historian': perhaps your childhood was puritanical and barren;

perhaps it was luscious, tender, and gay. A seemingly random sentence catches your eye, and resonates, arousing you to a particular time and place. You go into a daydream. Images reveal themselves, and then disappear. After a while, you become reabsorbed in the text, and warmed up to the 'Curious Learner' role once more. 'Does this writer have anything to say about groups that I want to hear?' you ask yourself.

You may observe that warm-up can simply mean that which readies you for a role or which occupies your psychic attention at the time. At its fullest, though, it is also a state of readiness for action, highly connected with spontaneity; this extra factor makes the example of you as reader an incomplete one. A fully warmed-up person asks: 'What must be done? What does the situation demand?' Maybe even 'asks' is the wrong word. When the warm-up is deepened, one recognizes clearly, second for second, that something is or is not being made. Feeling, thinking, and action flow into one another. Ambivalence is gone. A warm-up helps you go 'there' and start. The moment you accept going somewhere and starting, possibility is opened up, and the forbidden agendas, the restraints on doing something different, drop away.

Psychodramatists cheat a little on the 'proper' idea of warm-up, because sometimes they use the term to mean a continuous unfolding of roles, and at other times as an 'event', prior to and separate from something else. They are in fairly good company, because, as far as I can make out, Moreno himself, with characteristic freedom even from his own terminology, did the same. So one might hear novice leaders saying to each other: 'What shall we do for the warm-up tomorrow, Derek?' or 'In the warm-up exercise, we found that an amazing thing happened. . . .'. They are talking in a way that has become very common – warm-up as a 'thing' or set-piece has now taken over as the principal understanding of the term. So Derek and his pal are thinking in terms of 'starting off', getting the group 'loosened up' and ready to enact something. One must start off somewhere, of course – like anything else, this is just an endeavour put on by one poor lot of frail humans for another poor lot.

It seems a pity, however, to consider warm-up as an easy dumping-ground to describe 'anything that happens at the beginning of a session'. Whether the starters are physical or verbal, one hopes at the very least to develop enjoyment and group esprit. But even this wish is somewhat over-diffuse; it suggests that one can put on pretty well any exercise as long as it gets people hotted up and emotional. Warm-up in the action methods tradition, however, is closely related to role theory and to spontaneity. It is also related to planning: in a strategic action consultancy, directors attempt to create a learning environment that will lead to different perceptions and dissolve some of the forbidden agendas that operate within each individual and within the group as such. This assumes that they know, or are at least making good guesses at, what those restraints on spontaneity are. Starter warm-ups are designed to establish a structure within which the group may operate and an area of concern that will preoccupy the group's attention during the session.

The next four chapters are linked: the bulk of this one is devoted to group warm-up, concentrating on identity, relationship, and action; it will deal with warm-ups led by the director – ranging from apparently informal anecdotes to more structured group exercises around a certain theme. In later chapters, the leader's tasks and roles are outlined, and brief action sequences for contracting are explained. The 'why' of all this is called into question in the chapter called 'Warm-up to what?'. The final chapter in the series examines the limits of warm-up, and what you can do when there seems nothing to be done. It is called 'Failure in warm-up'. You can see from some of the chapter titles that the warm-up path is not always lined with roses. Nevertheless, let us make a start.

Group warm-ups – identity, regression, relationship, action

At the start of a group, people tend to be a little nervous about their new companions, and their place in the scheme of things. Consequently, they want to dissipate anxiety and send out something for others to respond to: to know others, and to be known. Before even speaking to each other, they are making decisions and choices about other people in the room. As you will see in the chapters on sociometry, Moreno thought that groups have an internal life of their own, and that this life can best be understood by examining the choices made at any moment with regard to each other (Fox, 1987, p. xiii). He insisted that every group has, underneath its visible structure, an internal invisible structure that is real, alive, and dynamic.

People need the chance to assess leaders in terms of their ability to do the job – expertness, attractiveness, and trustworthiness. The role of the leader and the leader's own warm-up to the task will be elaborated in later chapters. Next, people want some sense of *security*; this is best given by the formation of a real relationship with at least one other person in the group – see the section on 'small groupings' for a development of this notion. They want a chance to affirm their *identity*, too, and you will find ways of working with this wish. Because the group is an action group, members look forward (somewhat reluctantly, be it said), to the experience of being an *actor*; so ways must be found of getting them on stage in the first few hours while yet accepting their (understandable) *ambivalence* about being part of a group in the first place.

I have found that warm-ups involving at least some of the elements of identity, relationship, and action allow me and the group to establish our identities, to have fun, to become actors, and to prepare ourselves for a group where we can get things done. Sometimes the ways they get done may seem a little vulgar, but as Carl Whitaker said: 'God protect me from the person who makes believe they're not vulgar'.

In this chapter, several types of warm-up are outlined, and particular examples are given. The idea is that you will use the principles embedded in these examples (rather than directly the illustrated warm-ups themselves) to help run a lively and useful group. No matter how pragmatic a group's goals or how 'strategic' the methods of its leader, members need to be warmed up – to be involved, vital, and creative. Only then can they manage the transient psychological disruption of being in a group in the first place. How can this be achieved?

(a) Identity

Even the most highly task-oriented group, whose members are not apparently concerned with the 'self' in any therapeutic meaning of that term, has to surmount certain sociometric hurdles before its members can settle down fully. As you will see in the chapters on sociometry, whenever they are in society, people worry about their identity, their self-ness, and its relationship to structures of membership. This dialectic between the identity of individuals and their membership of a group persists throughout the life of the group, but changes form. The questions 'Do I fit in enough?'. . . . 'If I fit in too much, will I lose myself?' are never quite resolved.

Similar struggles go on in the course of other groups, such as families or work groups for most of their life-cycles: between the 'me' and 'me-as-a-member-of-this-family', or 'me' and 'me-in-this-organization'. Without something to belong to, we have no stable self; and yet complete attachment to any social unit implies a kind of annihilation of the self. Our sense of being a person derives from the ways we are drawn into a wider social unit, such as a nation, a profession, a family, or a learning group; our sense of uniqueness, or selfhood comes from the little ways in which we resist that pull.

At the very first session, a simple directive that captures identity issues may go something like this:

Say your name and say one thing about you. OR
Say your name and one thing about why you are here.

Such banal-sounding directives actually contain subtle and important messages, commands, and permissions. 'Say your name' reminds the person of their identity, and gives them a chance to assert it in the group. It also constitutes a kind of 'permission' for people to be individuals, and a recognition that their self-ness is important to hang on to in this new environment. 'Say one thing about you or 'Say one thing about why you are here' creates a search on the part of the members into what is preoccupying them at the time. Which physical characteristic, which anecdote, which daydream, which bit of their awareness will they select? The instructions contain an embedded command to search, and then to bring the 'inside' to the outside, the fantasy realm to the social realm. At the same time, the director is already gaining a sense of the themes that may be operating, of the 'group mind' that is already forming. If the group has been meeting for some time, directors might try a more 'advanced' form of identity warm-up:

How is what I am doing now a typical reaction to a new situation?
How is it different, if I had been in this situation a year ago?

You will by now have already picked up the 'news of difference' slant here. In fact, this simple identity warm-up achieves many goals at the individual level (though of course it does not actually *cause* relationships to commence, or even to become manifest if they already have commenced). Directors wish to shift the focus from identity to identity-in-relationship, given that identity is always in relationship or is implicitly defined against the identity of someone else. 'My name' is different from other people's names; 'one thing about me' is different from (or perhaps similar to – it is still a matter of relationship) other things about other people. Further to draw out the *relationship* nature of identity, therefore, the director might say:

Go over to the person who most/least sounded as if they would understand what it is that preoccupies you at the moment. OR

Go over to the person who most/least would have similar concerns to you.

Similarity and difference are the means by which we know who we are. Even at the beginning of a group, perceived similarities and differences between oneself and the other group members are of absorbing interest. A clique in a group, for instance, defines its members as being in some way 'alike', and 'not like the others'. Paradoxically, we most truly maintain our identity by contact with another. Martin Buber, who was an occasional contributor to a magazine that Moreno edited in the 1920s, maintained that the smallest unit is not one, but two: I-Thou. I cannot be I except in relation to Thou. Both poles are needed for identity: the 'I' needs to feel like a subject too, and in a group of strangers this 'I-ness' of me needs to be tightly held.

One of the best ways of dealing with members' temporarily fragile identities at the start of a group, therefore, is to build up both the 'I-ness' and the 'Thou-ness' of relationships: what Moreno calls *tele* relationships.

Directors can commence the building by asking members to form pairs in order to discuss something or other (a pair might be thought of as the smallest possible social atom necessary for survival). A typical instruction would go like this:

Get together with someone who you know relatively less well in the group, and talk to them for a minute or so about the simple pleasures of life. OR (for a work-based seminar)

Join someone you know relatively less well in the group, and talk to them for a minute about the simple pleasures involved in your job (director gives a few examples). OR

Form fours, and tell each other stories about your first day in the job. OR

Form fours, and tell each other stories about a student/employee who let you know that you need to know more about your job than you actually do.

These exercises are not only less threatening than to ask people to reveal something 'deep' about themselves, but they tend to lead to 'deeper' knowledge of one another anyway. People are not so 'defended' whilst talking about the 'simple pleasures of life', which might be a cigarette, a shower, a cup of tea, sitting down when one is tired, body surfing, or whatever. Or if they are only telling humorous stories about their first day at the job, etc., they will not look so bad – after all, everyone has such stories to tell. The revelation of humble detail about one's life and one's preferences is not so contrived or even so controlled as discussion of some private inner trauma might be. There seems to be no harm in letting the other person know these things; there seems to be no intrusion in learning about them from the other.

'Identity' warm-ups are helpful to protect the sense of self which is apparently under threat when one comes into a new group of people. If people's 'I-ness' is now acknowledged, they will tend to hang on to their identity so hard as to hamper them in their group activities. Creativity and spontaneity will be diminished, as people are afraid of exposing their identity to ridicule. Members will be afraid to take risks, to speak out, to be open to new thinking. Their capacity for learning, for surprise, for experimentation with new possibilities, is thereby greatly diminished.

Another 'identity' question simply gets the partners to describe how they got to the group that day; that is, how they physically travelled from their house to where the group is being held. The banal details involved in their descriptions give participants a very comfortable knowledge of each other, and also serve as a metaphor for the transition of 'home to here'. They link the person in the workshop with the person in that other place, thereby establishing them as having a 'real existence' outside this new social system. Yet the bridge between that other social system and this has been described in detail to another person who, as it turns out, has their own tale to tell.

Training Exercise: *Produce ten exercises for pairs based on identity ('this is me'). The exercises should be simple, and apparently 'non-psychological'. They should be appropriate to any group of people, teachers, managers, trainees in groupwork.*

(b) Regression

In the 1960s and early 70s, physical warm-ups became extremely popular. Numerous books on the market gave ready-made exercises and prescriptions for getting a group or a classroom buzzing. Some of the exercises had startling effects, at very little cost to the leader in terms of planning or conceptualizing. One simply took out a book, read an exercise, gave it to the group as one's own, and managed the consequences. It did not seem to matter which exercise was chosen: 'Oh well, so long as it gets them talking' or 'the hotter the better' appeared to be the philosophy. Experienced group members or befuddled students became quite used to instructions to 'Mill around, making eye contact', or 'Lie on the floor and become aware of the carpet'. And so they did.

Ethics aside, these methods bring with them certain difficulties, not the least of which is that the group can become warmed up precisely to the opposite state that the leader had intended. That is, a physical warm-up can easily evoke 'resistance' rather than release. That nice 'free-movement' warm-up can produce fear rather than disinhibition; the eye-contact game that the director had designed to foster intimacy arouses instead self-consciousness, isolation, and embarrassment. That innocuous milling exercise designed to break up sub-groups leads people to issues of distrust of authority because the leader 'tricked' them out of their secure friendship anchorages. The 'free drama' led to flatness instead of creativity and joy (the members felt not so much 'free' as that the leader was not able to create boundaries and purposes; they consequently became more frightened and 'defensive').

How can this be? Perhaps because after a while people have a good nose for a rat, especially when the rat has a large 'P' for psychology painted on it. In our heart of hearts we know that intimacy based on two minutes' encounter is not really going to lead up to the core of the universe. And when people feel too pushed, when the intended outcome is too obvious and too banal, they tend to be mistrustful and 'resistant'.

I am a little embarrassed to put this to you, because it seems so corny, but physical warm-ups (which Moreno, 1953, p. 338, calls 'bodily starters') can be fun. Games that involve competition and contest, such as simple chasing games, for example, warm people up to the best of amiability, laughter, and fellowship, rather than hostility and competitiveness. This amiable effect is somewhat paradoxical, given that such games are overtly competitive. In part the result may be due to the 'resistance' running the opposite way: that is, if people are more or less instructed to be competitive, the competitive roles in them are validated and exercised, leaving room for harmony and co-operation. Whereas if the competitive roles are ignored and exhortations are given to co-operate, those roles will perversely seek to be exercised. Perhaps the desirable effect also comes about because these games are not so 'corny', do not so much reek of 'psychology', do not have so many expectations behind them to be 'aware' as do more overt encounter-like warm-ups.

Carl Whitaker once remarked that the problem is not whether one is childish or not, but whether one is honest about being childish – we're all two years old. Whether or not we *are* two years old, we certainly can be. So a further reason why childhood games such as chasings, statues, Red Rover, Rats 'n' Rabbits seem to have better effects than the more sententious 'intimacy' exercises may be because they involve regression. While they seem silly and easy, they remind us or actually take us back ('regress us') to rather simpler times when we were children. Regression in psychiatry has got a bad name. But it seems that we throw out helpful regression, like happy playfulness, with unhelpful regression, like wetting the bed when we are forty.

To praise 'regression' is not to imply that all childhood experiences are happy. Many of the people in the group may have had a sorrowful childhood, inadequate parents, or cruel siblings. The regression involved in childhood games, however, does not usually evoke this side of childhood. In using a regressive game, the director is more likely to reach into a spirit of play, even for people who have rarely played. The creativity and simplicity involved in play are related to spontaneity. And since spontaneity is at the heart of the psychodramatic method, an exercise designed to generate playfulness can be a good place to start a psychodrama group.

Lastly, childish games often involve physical contact. For example, in the game of chasings, the chaser tries to 'tip' the quarry, and, as the game progresses, the various quarrys become more and more excited. They will duck behind other people in the room, bang into them in their efforts to escape, or cut corners, the 'corner' often being a person. These unthinking activities are more likely to provide acceptable avenues for breaking down sexual and other anxieties than clichéd intimacy games. The touching is unmindful, rapid, and with minimal sexual connotation. 'After all', the person can say, 'it's only a silly game'. This sort of activity is not designed to 'solve' any deep difficulties with sex or intimacy, and at some level participants may be aware of this innocence of purpose. The goal is short-term, social, and group-centred: to warm the group physically, and to ways of relating in which anything is possible – at least it makes people hot, puffing, and smiley. But it also provides an experience of child-like conviviality, spontaneity, and fraternal ease that becomes a base for the further therapeutic work of the group.

(c) Relationship

Action warm-ups are not confined to set games. Indeed, that is their minimal meaning in a psychodrama context. A true psychodramatic action warm-up involves the taking of roles as a result of a directive from the leader, or spontaneously, through development of the group's imagination. The instruction to action can be apparently frivolous, for example, 'Play Chasey', or more high-brow and serious, such as:

Put out the norms that you think will be present in this group.
Choose someone to be each of these norms.

The director then gets the people involved as 'the norms' to interact with each other, occasionally 'freezing' the action to make a comment. After this, the action of those 'on stage' can be spread back to relationships in the group by the director asking people to choose pairs and talk about what they have noticed. Here the warm-up 'formula' is to introduce a concept to members (such as, 'choose norms'), then one person sets out the various meanings of the concept, and finally members discuss the action in pairs. Another example of building a concept into a dialogue is this:

What are your regular life-giving roles? (Pairs) Come out to the stage and address your life-giving roles with the group as audience. What are the life-giving roles that are developing? Which ones would you like to develop?

If directors wished to transform the above to a didactic enactment, they could draw on a blackboard the speaker's role system that is emerging from their description, and ask people to comment.

The action could be taken even further, if desired, by having the person's parents (played by auxiliaries) stand somewhere in the area, so that they can be called on by the protagonist in terms of their relevance to the protagonist's 'life-giving roles' in the present. Naturally, if directors suggest that the parents stand *between* the protagonist and what they want, they are already setting up a structure of opposition, and inviting the protagonist to enter a warm-up involving anger. Such an action might well be reinforcing dysfunctional roles, such as 'Blamer' or 'Victim'. If, however, the parents are considered as relevant to the director for this exercise, and simply placed in a neutral position on stage, protagonists can make of them what they will. If *protagonists* choose to place parents between them and their goals, an oppositional enactment is in order.

Directors can easily make a name for themselves for incandescent warm-ups by setting up oppositional structures, but they may do so at ultimate cost to the members.

Another simple process that can increase the action state of the group is to expand an inner state into an outer state. Here are four alternatives for this type of activity. The instructions are given to the whole group:

Close your eyes and experience whatever emotions you have at the moment. Doesn't matter if they're frivolous and light, or dark and heavy. Now . . . where *are you? Put yourself in a landscape. OR*

(As above, except) when *did you have this feeling most strongly before? Set up the scene. OR*

Put a sound to the emotions you are feeling right now. Make that sound bigger, bigger, bigger. Now put words on it. Who *are you saying them to?*

Take a body posture as you are feeling right now. Exaggerate that posture . . . Now . . . who is there with you?

The first of these exercises uses the simple device of putting a geography on the imagination. The second is an invitation to link the present feeling with similar ones in the past, and to perform a brief enactment. The third and fourth exaggerate something that is already happening, but insist on the experience being interpersonal.

Set up two chairs, one to represent 'Where I am with me'; another to represent 'Where I am with you'. Put a person in each of those chairs, and find a physical correlate of their state, exaggerate it and begin talking to each of them.

There are other ways to link the here-and-now of the person's functioning in the group with the there-and-then of their functioning in the social atom. These can be ways to warm people up to a psychodrama itself, if that is what the group is for:

Draw a picture as you are today (allow five minutes or so). Now superimpose people from your family of origin. Pick a partner and discuss how you would use the picture in a drama. OR

You're all in relationships already with people in this group. Close your eyes and think for a minute with whom do you block yourself and with whom do you go free. Show your partner how you block someone with your eyes . . . with your voice . . . with your body. Now show your partner how you do this with relationships outside the group.

Using chairs, set out what your goals are in this group. . . . Now add, subtract, or re-arrange any chairs that refer to your life goals.

So far, we have been highlighting the function of the 'set' warm-up. Psychodramatists, however, seldom rely on the set warm-up beyond the first few sessions of a group. They ask themselves 'warm up to what?' For immediacy it is difficult to beat utilizing 'chance' statements of the group members or responses from a member to the director to increase the action component in the group. These opportunistic entries to action are often preferable to using a set exercise from the director. The skill is to see the potential action component of people's speech, and to regard what they say about themselves as an implicit dialogue with someone else. Once there is dialogue, there is drama as soon as the dialogue is moved to the stage area. Dialogue that takes place in the circle of the group is, of course, narrative (telling about something), or encounter (telling it to a group member, but not on stage). If a person says, for example, that they feel 'isolated', the director can reply:

From what? Who does the isolating? Choose someone to be that which isolates you, and that from which you are isolated.

Or the director can 'spread' the individual warm-up around the group, making the action first sociometric. In this case, the original person's statement is used as a warm-up for other members, and the sociometric soundness of the statement as a theme is tested out.

That sounds pretty terrible. Has anyone in the group felt like that in the past year?

and the the teller can be invited to a psychodramatic enactment:

What does . . . do that makes you feel isolated? What do you do in response to that? Who else apart from you and . . . is affected by your feeling isolated? . . . Sculpt the relationship between the three of you.

When people say they are 'stuck', a common psychodramatic device is to maximize the stuckness, and to give it a geography: 'Stuck in what? Stuck trying to get where, or away from whom? What is the substance like in which you are stuck?' But just as a person may be helped out of stuckness by increasing it, the opposite position can also be taken where the person is asked to enact a scene where he or she is *not* stuck. For the director to imply that they are not stuck *now* is inadvisable, as this will usually result in the protagonist feeling unengaged, and the director and protagonist begin to fight each other over an interpretation. A transcendent scene, however, where the protagonist has already learnt the roles necessary not to be stuck, may be played in the past or in the future. Sometimes it is helpful totally to have the scene as an unlikely fabrication, and to keep stressing the fantasy side of it. The usual result is that the person feels joined, and can move again, simply from having been an actor.

Is there a sound that fits at the moment?
Make that sound, no matter how faint, no matter how wavery. Now increase it a little. . . . That's too much – take it down a bit. Now bring it up a little more. Get someone here who may be attracted/repelled by that sound.

Here the director is changing mode. A mode that is depressed or stuck is often 'kinaesthetic'; overwhelming physical and emotional feelings make the person shut down or mute. By shifting to another mode, the auditory, still analogous to the physical (that is, a sound is asked for at first, rather than words), the kinaesthetic mode is by-passed. If the protagonist is responsive to the instructions about sound, the director and protagonist can keep playing with the medium until an image develops, or perhaps an animal sound emerges. The protagonist can then begin to act within that image or as that animal.

A similar procedure can take place if the person says that they feel 'guilty'. The guilty feeling itself can be made concrete by means of an auxiliary, or the person can be asked towards whom they feel guilty, and the guilt is then maximized. But a reversal can also take place. Instead of guilt always being treated as irrational, an emotion to be psychodramatically purged, the director can attend to the impulse behind the guilt, and have the protagonist ask the relevant other for forgiveness. Sometimes this way of tracking the 'invisible loyalties' to their source and there performing the appropriate rituals is sounder and more moving than applying conventional therapeutic wisdom that one should not be guilty towards anyone.

(d) Action

Action has been a theme of this whole book, as it is of the method itself. The discrete section presented here, then, is to be taken in the context of all that has been written so far, and is particularly devoted to the warm-up stages at the start of a session.

When group members are having some difficulty coming to terms with each other, or with being members in the first place, an effective warm-up is to ask each of them for a metaphor of the group ('This group is like. . . .'). So far, as you will recognize, this is fairly standard group practice. A litre or two of action rocket-fuel, however, launches members into productive areas, and makes the trip more enjoyable, too. It is not necessary to enact each member's statement; rather, directors can wait until someone makes a statement that quickens their own blood, or encapsulates a group theme, or has a suitable dynamic in it.

The group cannot seem to get going; members sit around in the doldrums. Dot asks them to think of a metaphor for themselves at the moment.

Members start to call out ideas – already things are livening up. (Reader, if you are from a certain tradition, you may be dismayed at Dot for not going into the dynamics of why *they are so sad and stuck on this occasion.)*

Marty says that the group is like a rubber ball pressing against a grid, and sandwiched by the earth below. Dot asks Marty to choose a member to be the grid, the ball, the earth, and then to watch the enactment, using role reversal in the usual manner.

She then asks the whole group to break into threes, being ball, earth, and grid, and to take turns being each. The group breaks out into tigerish delight as the ball, sadism as the grid, and solidity as the earth. Each person gets a chance to be each element.

Having people become actors cuts across their usual way of establishing themselves, and requires them to find new ways of structuring their social world. The action itself is the first lesson in spontaneity. Before action is interaction. The way to it is to get people to share their awareness of how they experience themselves. The director encourages this process, promotes crossfire, listens empathically, and leads as quickly as possible to the enactment. When a group central concern is expressed (see Buchanan, 1980, and *The Passionate Technique*, Chapter 3), one can launch immediately into action, confident that the action will be relevant to the whole group, and that the change in the protagonist will imply a change in the group itself.

The demented chook

Mollie is enacting a drama on how her boss intimidates her. A scene in the office is set up, with the boss sitting on his high-backed executive chair behind a big desk. He acts pretty pleased with himself, picking his nose and smoothing down his lapels. Mollie enters, and a dialogue ensues, in which the boss is rude to Mollie, and she is cowed. She tells the director that she 'just flaps around like a demented chook' when she gets into these types of situations. The director suggests that Mollie do just that.

Mollie dances around the boss's desk, flapping her arms and making noises like a crazed chicken. The boss is laughing, the group is laughing; Mollie and the director are not laughing. Suddenly she changes, and starts to bang the boss's table, demanding that he treat her seriously. She goes right over the top of the desk, and topples him out of his big fat chair; he ends up on the floor, with the chair on top of him. Mollie sits on his chest and has 'a few quiet words' with him about their working relationship, after which the vignette ends.

The next week she returns to the group and tells the members that she has said 'no' to a couple of the boss's demands, and that his attitude towards her has changed considerably. When asked how she had managed this new behaviour, Mollie replies that it had 'just slipped out; it was easy. I didn't think. It was only little things he wanted, but it just wasn't right for me to do them and I just said the first thing that came into my head.'

So here we are at warming up to a role again. You see the process is circular – from group-as-a-whole warm-up to warming up to a role, and then to group-as-a-whole again. When Mollie warms up to the role of a 'demented chook', neither she nor the group for one moment imagine that her actions are a direct rehearsal for behaviour in the office on the following Monday. Nor is her struggle with the boss, throwing him to the floor and sitting on his chest a life-like run through of what she will later do. But all these actions are important, as Mollie deepens her warm-up to the frenzied internal state (demented chook) that she experiences every working day, and which is very painful for her. If she can give full rein to this, all stops out, new possibilities may emerge which could surprise her. And so, after Demented Chook is enacted, another role emerges, namely that of 'Amazon' or indomitable fighter. This one, too, is fully experienced, and she changes to 'Powerful Negotiator', though there is still a large element of fantasy (after all, she is sitting on the boss's chest). 'Reality and fantasy are not in conflict', says Moreno (1953, p. 82): in its logic, the ghost of Hamlet's father is just as real and permitted to exist as Hamlet himself. On stage fantasy can become flesh, and be given equal status with perceptions usually labelled as 'normal'.

Chapter seven

Finding a voice

Finding a voice means that you can get your own feeling into your own words and that your words have the feel of you about them.

Seamus Heaney

Theme introduction

Finding a voice differs from learning a technique: technique is what you can learn from reading, from training, and from supervision. Technique can be deployed, sometimes at least, without reference to the feelings or to the self – you just do the job. Don't get me wrong: one practises a technique, and mimes the real thing, until a voice is found. A 'voice' is one's stance on life, one's own definition of reality. It cannot be taught. When directors have found a voice, they can 'raid the inarticulate', as Heaney (1980) would put it; they can mediate between the origins of feeling in memory and experience and the formal technique that expresses these in the aesthetics and pragmatics of a drama. Directors who have found a voice are able to bring the meaning of experience within the jurisdiction of form (see final chapter). They help the protagonist move from incoherence to something intended and complete; and they use themselves to help group members be in touch with what is there, hidden and real, in the warm-up that each of them brings to the group.

Directors can warm up a group by initiating a theme themselves, perhaps by personal anecdote. The talk gives them an early opportunity to disclose some of their own style, and have the group make reality-based links to them. When directors are talking at the beginning of a group, they themselves make a 'leap into the void', fighting their own shyness and desire to retreat, knowing that they are being sized up by a group of unknown people. The group members, too, when it is their turn to become actors, will also experience this void, the feeling of creating each moment. The sense of void in front of one is much greater when one is an actor-talker rather than simply a talker. By stepping before anyone else into the void, directors create a 'container' where group members can let go their past certainties: it becomes acceptable to lose the security of knowing ahead of time what is going to happen.

A theme introduction needs to steer between these two poles of being adequately general and 'psychological', and yet sufficiently attending to the presenting focus, the overt purpose of the group's meeting. Sometimes it may take the form of anecdote or personal story. When directors do tell such a story, they hope to trigger a personal exploration that is relevant to the theme of the group. If 'learning' is the theme, they may start the group by talking about a situation that they themselves have been in where the way they learnt was at issue. They may talk about a recent experience, a situation that is still alive, and possibly still unresolved. The purpose of the story is to trigger participants' recollection of their own experience at a similar point in learning.

Colliver (1987) suggests that an effective personal story needs to have five characteristics: firstly, it must be about something with which participants can identify because it falls within their life experiences. Secondly, it must touch on the leader's thinking/feeling states and actual behaviour as he or she responded, thus allowing participants to resonate with one of these modes too. Thirdly, maintains Colliver, a personal story needs to relate to external events, moving between the experience of the teller, the context, and the other people involved. Inner experience on its own will not do. A story can provide a good model for systems exploration, suggesting a process of enquiry into both external and internal events, and their interaction.

Fourthly, an appropriate story will illustrate the various roles and attempted solutions that the teller accesses to deal with the situation. These roles and states can be designed to parallel likely similar states in the group with which members are struggling – panic, repeated solutions, self-criticisms, and so on. Lastly, the story stops before the resolution – at the point where people are asking themselves 'What would I do now?' The idea of the story is to open a state of question and exploration, rather than to illustrate a teaching point or to recommend a guide. After the story, participants are invited to respond: 'What would you have done?' 'Are you often in a situation like this one?' and so on. The leaders are especially interested in participants' different ways of responding – the different roles that are evoked. At the same time, social connectedness is encouraged, and a group norm of acceptance of difference is established.

The type of story told depends on the purposes of the group. Where these are general, such as 'to learn about psychodrama', or the more global goals of a personal growth or therapy group, directors may be a little broader in their scope, and also more overtly personal and 'psychological'. Members will almost certainly be aroused by stories that contain themes such as 'setting out', 'an adventure', 'new learning', or 'inclusion'. The leader's talk or series of anecdotes on these themes provides a structure so that people can think around definite themes, but it is not so definite that members will feel constrained, pushed, and needing to fight to maintain their sense of autonomy.

'Universal themes' are those with which all members of the group can make contact. Virtually everyone has some experience of shyness, death, being adventurous, night-time, first day at school, prejudice, playing, feeling excluded, being comforted, and the like. The talk is a window to the psychology of certain crucial situations (adventure/defeat, for example) that get repeated over and over in everyday life, but which have been beaten down, ignored, or forgotten; the talk provides an occasion for members to reflect on their interaction with such issues. As a result, the group tends to 'connect' with the director, and begins to form a real relationship with him or her. They also 'connect' with themselves and their own warm-up to the issues.

All going well, the members understand the actual and possible relations these situations being recounted might have with other aspects of their lives. The warm-up talk heightens their sense of their own functioning. The issue becomes alive for them; it may even become urgent, leading them to become actors. Their sense of their own life, their vital forces, becomes sharper. They reflect on the theme, whether a work-based theme or a therapy theme, as part of living reality rather than something remembered and applied. Consequently, they begin to have a sense of excitement and apprehension of the unknown. In short, the talk heightens, underlines, signifies, symbolizes, initiates this time as a time when people can act differently. It creates an atmosphere of 'Anything can happen'.

It helps if the director *values* small things, and so develops a sense of naivety and wonder in the group members, who begin also to value small gestures, thoughts, and movements. Feelings of mutual worth and of self-worth are enhanced. No matter how 'strategic' or goal-oriented a group is, these qualities are indispensable for change and invaluable in themselves. The director's own mood and style of speech are cardinal, since his or her very first comments act as a warm-up to a particular state – to trust or confidence or fear or lightness or aggression. Despairing or negative directors have no trouble in evoking symmetrical or complementary states in the group: members will themselves become despondent or maniacally positive. Likewise, stuck and censorious directors tend at least to flatten any spontaneity that would otherwise have been possible; if the group reaction becomes complementary, members may indulge in cycles of outrageous acting out, followed by penitence, followed by more 'intolerable' behaviour.

Because of the amount of personal exposure involved in their work, directors may need to spend some time on their own warm-ups prior to the group. When one feels competent and trustworthy, one enjoys the job so much more. A director then can be 'a human being' in the group, experiencing personally the impact of each member. Directors who roughly know what they are doing and what they are going to do are able to become aware of the links between themselves and the members of the group and to act on them, making them overt. It is a marvellous feeling when one gets to a point of competence where at least the technical difficulties are long behind. Then one can live fully while directing, just as a well-practised singer does not have to look at the notes or scowl at the music sheet any more, but can focus on the meaning of the piece itself. With command of technique, one can find one's voice, and use it.

Customership

Part of the director's own warm-up time is used to review the group's most recent themes and concerns. The director goes over the contractual arrangements so far made – the specific goals and purposes for which the group was formed. The question as to why each person has come is relevant, and so is the question 'Why now?' These questions get at the warm-up of each person to his or her issues, and allow the director to see something of the context of the problem. In the case reported below Con, the consultant, is up against the difficulty of customership, except that this time there is *too much* customership – for another person to change, that is. Somehow he has to get the company to which he is consulting to drop their habitual solutions and have a different *kind* of look at the problem.

Angie's ambivalence

A theatre company seeks help because it is having trouble with Angie, one of its actors. Angie seems to be ambivalent about being a member of the company, cannot meet important commitments, is unable to attend rehearsals, etc., because of a new relationship she has formed. Company members, and the head of the company, are tearing their hair out with rage at Angie. At the same time, they are terrified that she will leave. They fear her departure will deprive them of one of their best talents, and will also be a kind of judgement on them all.

Being somewhat psychologically-minded, the company puzzles on the meaning of all this: Should they be angry with her and provoke fights? Should they just throw her out? The head volunteers that Angie's shifting in and out might be 'a metaphor for the company's shifting in and out of commitment to me'.

The consultant, Con, notes these and other explanations as part of the company's attempted solutions, and signifying their very involvement with the problem. Primarily, and naturally enough, they want him to 'fix up' Angie.

Con asks Jim, the head of the company, how Angie's behaviour is a problem. Jim is first of all surprised that Con would even ask such a question. After all, it was obvious why it was a problem. Nevertheless, he has trouble answering this 'obvious' question, and says that he 'would have to handle all the anger'. And how is that a problem? asks Con. Jim thinks again. 'Because they are getting so angry that they cannot work.' This, then, becomes the problem that Con and the company work on – not Angie's presumed defection, but how to work effectively while they are angry. Con then asks how long this problem has been around, and who it most affects. He tries to divine the relative influence (White, 1986) of the problem on the company versus the relative influence of the company on the problem. This discussion goes on for a while (not reported here). In a short time, the company 'forgets' to be angry with Angie, and she begins to come to rehearsals on time.

Sometimes a group's goals are quite specific, such as those subscribed to by a phobia group, a smokers' group, or an obesity group. Other types of groups are specific in their end point, while leaving a lot of flexibility as to means, as in a psychodrama training group. Here the aim is to be trained and adequate professionals, but it is usually understood that this training involves 'personal work' as well as technical expertise. Obviously the group design must fit the population it serves: the mixture of open discussion, structured exercises, amount of appropriate exploration of the past via action methods, didactic input, and so on, needs to be tailored to the population that the group is serving.

Sometimes the *goals* of the group are not specific, but the *means* are fairly well understood: a psychotherapy group for people with mixed difficulties, such as anxiety, depression, sexual problems, shyness, or obsessive difficulties might make up such a mixed group. At the outset, members' goals would be generally to 'get better' or 'to grow'. The means may or may not initially be fully understood, but most people would realize that group interaction is involved. From this interaction, group norms will develop, though they may remain unspoken. When the goals of a group are too diffuse and too unspoken, there is little opportunity to see whether they are being met. One can never quite tell whether one has 'got there', and consequently the group meets for as long as it meets, and it stops when it is 'time to stop', rather than when its aims have been achieved. Personal growth groups, for example, often have a time to stop – usually about eight to ten weeks – rather than a target for stopping. When customership is so diffuse, one needs to beware that the group does not become a no-change ratification for the seriousness of one's problems, and the impossibility of their resolution.

When there is only a time for stopping (rather than a goal for stopping) it is much more difficult to have a 'news of difference' agenda, because the group is not set up to do anything more than 'run for a few weeks' or 'help people develop themselves more fully'. A target for stopping might be arranged in the first two sessions. Such a target in itself helps people (including the director) to be serious about change and to assess difference over time. It increases customership (de Shazer, 1988) in the group, or at least makes it overt who are customers and who are not. It is easy to be too idealistic in this matter, however, and consultants often have to settle for what they can get. This is especially so if they are called in to 'fix' an ailing group which has little desire to be 'fixed'. Then the problem is one of the referring person (for a fuller explanation of this point, see Selvini Palazzoli *et al.* (1980) and Williams (1989b).

Even if the goal of the group is diffuse, such as 'to improve my personal relationships' or 'to explore my standing with others', these goals need to be alluded to frequently within the group, and taken seriously in terms of how the group-as-a-whole and each individual member is meeting them. 'How are your personal relationships different from two weeks ago? With whom would you most want them to change? What would your relationship be like if it did change?' are questions that track difference and also bring it about. People often change their aims as a series of sessions progresses. This seems reasonable, even commendable, as other issues gain salience. But the old goal can still be used as a lever:

What is it like not to have X as a goal any more?
What is your experience as you come to terms with this now?

People may come with several problems but choose to work on the most bothersome first. If that one is eliminated or becomes irrelevant, they go on to the second, and the third, and so on down the line. Or they may take an easier and less embarrassing problem first. This too is acceptable: having a hierarchy of problems does not of itself suggest failure in the wish to solve any problems. The very ordering of them is helpful, and is the beginning of customership. The procedure of drawing attention to the differences, however, still applies. Events within the group, no matter how dramatic or important in their own right, need to be related back to the original purpose:

Since the drama a few weeks ago, Alfie, what has changed for you in terms of your heavy drinking? How much is the role of Hopeless Drunk winning over the role of Little Battler?

The art with contracting is to maintain and use the contract as a milestone for progress, yet not have it so specific that the group will want to resist the contract. Milestones, not millstones.

Preoccupying concerns and frontiers

Several forms of double description suggest themselves when one considers a person entering a group. For example, any number of now/future exercises can be constructed around the person's level of entry – where they are now and where they want to be at the end of the group. Whitaker (1985) calls a 'preoccupying concern' the issues, life events, or responsibilities that have led the person to the group in the first place.

Directors focus on individuals in the group in a manner that connects them to the original purpose of the group. The simplest ways are sometimes the most effective in this. For example, if the theme is quitting smoking, the director can then ask 'What's quitting like for you? For you? And you?' etc. They may link the current theme with the original purpose for entering the group ('preoccupying concern') for each member. Everybody in the group needs to feel 'joined' in some way: if only a few members are concentrated upon, this practice will strongly affect the feeling in the group, with certain people experiencing themselves as isolated, less interesting, or failures.

The first double description is done by persons working in pairs; participants are asked to note something as simple as 'Hopes' for workshop outcomes: 'By the end of this workshop I want to be able to . . .' versus 'Fear' of workshop outcomes: 'I fear the workshop will not succeed in . . . .' Their partners are asked to listen for a view that is interesting, but dissimilar to their own (thereby creating a further double description). The move from here to action is easy: members can select a chair for 'Hope' and a chair for 'Fear', and address these separate entities. The hope and fear can concern the processes of the workshop itself, which are often frightening to people not used to news of difference being brought by means of action.

According to Whitaker (1985), a 'frontier' marks the boundaries between the understandings, skills, and personal resources which members have, and those which they do not have. In the early stages of a group it is relevant to elicit the preoccupying concerns, either by conversation, empty chair, or by sociometry. The 'frontier', however, is especially amenable to dialectical treatment, because, as with the notion of self, a frontier is a place between somewhere and somewhere else. An imaginary line can be drawn in the room and the director says:

Each of you imagine this line . . . on this side is the you as you are now, with the skills and abilities you have now. On the other side is the you with the skills and abilities you expect to gain as a result of this group.

The director gets the whole group to stand on one side of the line and to go over for themselves the qualities they think that they bring to the task, and the position that they are in then and there. Members are asked to talk to themselves silently. Then they are asked to cross the line, and talk to themselves in the possession of their new skills.

If the group seems shy, the director might leave it at that. Most of the work has been done in any case. But if people seem even half way confident, members can be sat down, and individual members can stand and speak out loud their two sets of dialogue. When a person is in the second position (that is, of having achieved what they wanted) the director can ask them how they got there. In this way the actual path to creativity is set out by each member. The 'dramatic' element can be tuned up or down as required – that is, dialogue between the two parts can be introduced, and significant gestures or elements can be expanded or maximized.

The dilemma of change itself can be part of a dialectical reformulation. Individuals and organizations that seek the assistance of a group generally do so because of difficulties and discomfort for which they have been unable to find a solution. The solution, as we have seen, is the third part of a traditional dialectic. Strategic therapy's main method is to investigate the solutions that have been attempted to these difficulties. One usually finds that these attempts at solutions have served to perpetuate and even reinforce the very problems they were intended to solve (Watzlawick *et al.*, 1974; Fisch *et al.*, 1982). Even though these solutions do not 'work', they are resorted to time and again. Some alternative solutions, apparently different because apparently opposite, may have been attempted, and these too may have been applied more and more forcefully, even though success has not been indicated. Alternative solutions are 'forbidden' to appear.

Planning

A leader sets the warm-up according to: the people who constitute the group's membership; the purpose of the group; the number of times it has met (first time, second time, etc.); the number of times it is going to meet, whether circumstances demand it is time-limited rather than outcome-oriented. Is it a one-off group, such as a seminar? A six-session group, such as a weekend workshop? A consultancy that finishes when the job is done? The initial tasks and problems are rather similar, though they would be approached with greater or less degrees of elaborateness appropriate to the time that the group is meeting.

Irrespective of the time allotted, groups based on action methods would probably have these objectives in common:

(a) To establish conditions where learning will occur.
(b) To increase mutual trust and to allow opportunity for connections to develop among participants.

(c) To release spontaneity in the group so that the members will be open to creativity.
(d) To introduce action early on, so that group members begin to identify themselves as 'actors'.

Now the task becomes to meet these purposes competently. How does one start? A simple way to plan a series of sessions is to reverse roles with the forthcoming audience: what are likely to be the common grounds, the formal and informal issues that will bring them there? What are the limitations and resources available? What is the history (if any) of the group? To what role clusters does the director wish to warm the group – for example, Competent Administrator; Novel Thinker; Planner; Creative Artist?

Just asking these questions usually provides clues to the design of the opening sessions. The director might choose a role that is common to the incoming group: they are all city engineers, say, or all Repetitive Strain Injury sufferers, or all patients, or all psychodrama trainees. Now one can ask questions about the natural warm-up to the social aspects of this role? In role reversal, the question might be 'Will I be afraid or pleased to see other people? Will I be glad of a break, or resentful of this intrusion into my personal or professional time?' The questions might then go to the personal aspects of the incoming role: 'What am I hoping will happen for me? What will I make of this method or process?' And finally, directors can turn their attention to the *professional* aspects of the incoming role (if applicable): 'Will this be a waste of time? Will I get what I want in terms of solving these problems at work? Will this be the same old stuff? Is this leader competent?'

Let us imagine that the incoming group are all professionals at a work-sponsored residential seminar; in fact, they are the vice-principals of a region's high schools. Since they have all been put together for their annual two-day seminar, they might personally be feeling pleased to have a break, be missing home, and be a little wary of the leader. Professionally, they are curious about the content of the seminar, and eager to learn new methods to deal with certain difficulties at their schools. At the social level, they may feel competitive with all these people on the same level as themselves; they may also be hoping that the other members of the seminar will like them.

The simple and commonsense answers derived from the imagined role reversal 'to what roles would I be warmed up if I were coming here today?' provides a key to designing successful introduction procedures that are relevant to the new participants and the purpose for which they have come. The warm-ups can cover some or all of the areas of competition, delight at having a break, curiosity, desire for new methods, and the hope for amiability and friendship. The director validates these states implicitly or explicitly, and sets boundaries for the meeting, such as its purpose and the tasks requiring to be done. When a group meets knowing what its purpose is, its productivity will tend to rise and so will its spontaneity.

The warm-up exercises need simultaneously to cater for personal and professional reasons for attendance. I have listed below some exercises that progressively become more advanced, and demand more of the participants. They are intended as examples of warm-ups that would make professional sense to people (so that they do not feel indignant or cheated) and yet require a degree of personal involvement. They are intended to be done in conjunction with sociometric activities directly involving them as group members (which will be detailed later). The director might say:

List all the roles that you have at work . . . (allow time). Put a mark opposite those where you feel little or no conflict. Now put a mark alongside those where you feel the most conflict. In which role do you feel the most conflict of all? Mark it and tell your partner. Later we might do some work out the front here with a few of those that you all have in common. OR

Write on a card one major role of a vice-principal (explains what a major role is) that conflicts with another major role. OR

Think of significant teachers who have influenced you. We've got the opportunity today to bring just a few of those teachers into this group. (Stands behind a chair.) How about one of you puts one of those long gone teachers into this chair and has a conversation with him. Here, I'll show you how to do it. OR

Go to your late adolescence. Who were the people influential in making a choice about the profession you are in? Draw a social atom of that. I'll show you how to do it on the blackboard, and I'll tell you what I mean by 'social atom'. OR

What are the positive rituals that take place in your workplace, and what are the negative rituals? Draw up a list and show them to your partner. Afterwards we'll see what is common. OR

Write down the roles you would like to star in at work. What skills do you need, what presentation do you need to be highly chosen?

The final exercise that is detailed below is quite sophisticated, and would not be used on the first day of a seminar. In this exercise, the director writes on the board some of the work roles of the participants – Meeter, Joiner, Strategist, Manager, Clarifier, Rubber Stamp, etc., and asks participants to call out more of them. When the list is quite large, these are the instructions:

Score these for yourself on a one to five scale. See how your scores cluster. Discuss this with your partner. Select certain ones at the extremes of the scale, and show your partner how they fit in with your original social atom. Have mother make a statement to father: father to mother. Now both of them to you.

Taking off

Many leaders find that the hardest part of running a group is starting off. Similarly, it is said that a 747 pilot's greatest difficulties are in take-offs and landings. The actual flight (once the group is working on its tasks) is relatively easy. But will the plane have sufficient lift? Is it going in the right direction against the wind? Will it be able to land again safely? Analogously, these are more difficult judgements for many directors than actually directing a short action piece or even a longer drama – the mid-flight period where everyone is actually 'up'. Here follows a list with eight items on it of what the leader has to do at the take-off stage. Actually, there are even more dials to check, but this schedule is already intimidating enough for the moment. Leaders are required:

1. *To set a framework for the group, such as how long it will last, what its general purposes are, and what kind of group it is.*
2. *To clarify the tasks of the group and to assist members to clarify their expectations of the group.*
3. *To establish, and to model, where appropriate, norms for acceptability of action, spontaneity, and forceful expression.*
4. *To develop rapport and engagement with individual members and with the group as a system.*
5. *To develop group cohesion and a working basis of mutual trust between members.*
6. *To reassure the group of their expertise, their ability to warm up the group, and to manage safely what emerges as a result of the warm-up.*
7. *To accept reserved and shy behaviour; toleration of distance and difficulty indicates respect for members and reassures them that they are not expected to be 'group clones'.*
8. *To begin a process of information-exchange, whereby new meanings are able to be ascribed to present and past behaviour.*

If one had to boil this list down to three factors, they would probably be these: directors need to engender confidence that appropriate administrative and professional functions will be performed. Secondly, they engage with each individual and with the group system as a whole, joining members at their level of meaning to find out what the problem (or training need) is. Thirdly, they pave the way for new meanings to be possible. Essentially, they provide a setting within which the group can survive transient psychological disruption – a group climate safe enough that new information can be absorbed, and not so safe that there will be no challenge to existing structures.

The whole group, leader and members alike, will benefit from an emotional and intellectual experience that leads to a sense of pride and self-satisfaction, rather than shame and self-doubt. Directors warm up to this event, too, since after all they have the same task in life as each member – to react as spontaneously as possible to their lived experience, to become alive to the demand of this moment, and respond to it as adequately as possible.

Spreading the warm-up

At the start of a group, leaders are highly salient to all members. Later, that will change, and peers become more important. Members taking responsibility for their own learning is an admirable goal, but it is not usually achieved first-up, nor by taking away people's sense of structure. A group is a social organization convened by an authority, a paid professional with designated leadership roles; it is unfair to 'pathologize' the confusion that ensues if these roles are denied. Leaders who simultaneously take on this role and abnegate it understandably create bewilderment and regression amongst the members. If this state is then used against the members, perhaps to reinforce their already strong feelings of inferiority, they tend to become more, rather than less dependent, and more ready to be self-castigating under the guise of openness or awareness. Secondary victimization begins.

The first day of a group, then, provokes a strong dependency dynamic. The members believe, quite reasonably, that if they are going to get what they want, it will be from the leader, rather than from other group members. That is why the leader needs to create a situation that is familiar enough so that people will not feel discouraged, and yet is strange enough for them to feel that something new may happen. Even the most competent group simultaneously wants the leader to provide the solutions to its problems, and yet wants to develop those solutions itself. Rather than seeing this apparent contradiction as an attempt to disqualify the leader, it can be recognized as a part of the group's competence in asking for 'outside' help. They want no more help than is absolutely necessary, however. The slow process of directing the resources of the group back on itself now begins.

For leaders to refer to the 'group dynamic' at this stage is pointless, even sadistic. Such remarks set the group members up at best as little psychologists, and at worst as 'dummies'. In the early hours of a group people do not care about 'the group dynamic', and nor should they. As far as they are concerned, structure is going to come from the centre. To be sure, the 'group dynamic', that is, the system of interconnecting beliefs and roles, is already embryonic, and even at this stage has the potential to be a helpful or harmful force. This is a complicated matter, and group-as-a-whole interventions suitable for a group in progress will be discussed more fully in the chapters on sociometry.

A nice, long, hot psychodrama in the early stages would do much to enhance the director's charismatic power. But although gratifying for the director, and something of a relief for the members who have the equivalent of television to watch instead of going about the painful task of forming relationships, early enactment of a long drama is sociometrically unsound. 'Histrionic' or compliant members may warm up early, seize the time of the group, and then be envied or possibly ostracized for having done so. Their drama may itself be flat and unauthentic-seeming, though it appeared to begin with a high pitch of warm-up. Even if sometimes their psychodrama provides an excellent demonstration of the method, 'there may be little closure and/or sharing, and the sociometry position may not ensure an on-going support system' (Buchanan, 1980, p. 50).

The second difficulty that a precocious psychodrama can cause concerns the group itself: an early hierarchy of therapy savants may be established, whose notions of how a group 'should be' can become part of the group's rigid thinking. A director needs to create structures whereby in the early stages several people become actors in the sessions, or where the action is spread through the group itself, rather than focused on one person for a large amount of time. Empty chair work is one of the avenues for this sociometric diaspora, but there are many others. For instance, consider the following simple exercise which some directors frequently use for beginning a group:

Get into pairs and discuss with each other very briefly how you are in the group at this moment. Using your partner as yourself, sculpt him or her according to the way you feel now. OR

Tell your partner how you feel and have him or her sculpt you according to their impressions.

Later these sculptures can be shown to the group as a form of self presentation. This way, a norm is established that everyone is an actor, as well as being a talker or feeler. The shared confidences and the requirements to move around and take up space in themselves tend to build in a horizontal support system, which makes the basic assumption shift away from dependency. When the support system is spread through the group, the notion that the only way one can get support is through 'authorities', that is, the director and analogously, perhaps, one's parents, is undermined. Spreading the action also deals with the isolation dynamics in the group. When they are actors, in however limited a fashion, even the shyest people become visible, have a public face. The message is 'You don't have to be a star to be in this show'.

Participants tend to relax and feel they are in safe hands when group warm-up exercises are well designed, that is, when they are personally intriguing and professionally relevant. Only then can members let go some of their suspicion about these strangers with whom they have been cast for a period of time, and begin to form real links with two or more other people, depending on their general level of extroversion and personal style. With luck, the group is lively, willing to be surprised, and already in a small way accustomed to being actors rather than simply consumers. Be patient – this atmosphere and these skills take a little time to build.

Chapter eight

Warm-up to what?

It seems strange, but not uncommon, how one's legs go from under one when the mind's in pain.

Kate Llewellyn

In the state of spontaneity, decisions and changes of orientation tumble over one another. We get lost, in order to find ourselves. Ultimately, change eventuates from an altered epistemology, our pattern of perceiving and knowing. But the process by which this is done, by which restraints drop away, need not be known. The point of change is best achieved if interactional forces are deeply experienced by those participating in the enactment; this involvement can be called warm-up.

Like it or not, warm-up runs through a group all the time, just as it does in an individual. Not formal warm-ups put on by the director, of course, but the warm-up to roles that each individual has, and that the group-as-a-whole has. That is, the group can act as an individual, and be warmed up to a role, with or without a formal process preceding this. Indeed, it is often warmed up to just the opposite sort of role from the one the director thinks it 'should' be warmed up to. But that is another story, which will be told in the next chapter, and in subsequent ones on sociometry.

The question, then, can never be whether to 'have' a warm-up or not, but what is the most helpful way to use what is already there, or how to introduce a new direction. A formal warming-up process is designed to get the group members alive to the function of the group, to be caught up by the process of living. When well done, it widens the group's perceptions of what is possible, and starts members interacting more directly with others. The resulting generalized state of arousal and disinhibition pays off later when the action phase of the group occurs. Members are more likely to enter interactions as events in the present, rather than as a deadened re-creation of something from another time. Their auxiliary work has more zest, and solutions to problems tend to be more wide ranging and looser.

These are fine qualities, to be sure, and no group will stay together for long without most of them appearing on the menu. Without them, the group will lose cohesion, and therefore customership. Lacking sap, the tree withers, no matter how much 'good work' is being done at the base, or how carefully it is espaliered. Spontaneity, action, interaction are as necessary for problem-solving as they are for the group to live. Somehow these have to be nurtured, while the purpose of the group also has to be kept in mind. Some task, eh? – enough to set anyone's mind in pain. Who would condemn a director whose legs sometimes 'go from under'?

I am suggesting that strategic consultants ask not only questions of 'how to do it' about warm-up (which are hard enough sometimes) but also this question about warm-up: 'Warm-up to what?' The question can often be an embarrassing one; no wonder it is sometimes asked only in a whisper, or not at all. Warm-up, for strategic directors, means more than arousal. They hope to promote new roles, to introduce new meaning by having the group members become alive to, and then redefine problematic behaviour. They usher in the type of events and actions where the need for new meanings is evident, and the opportunity to obtain them is provided.

Dorrie

Are you alone? Are you in silence? Even so, your 'reality' is bombarded enough, just with reading accounts of groups, far less conducting them. In the hurly burly of a group, stories about 'what happened' and even 'what is happening' do not remain static. Group members continually react with each other and with the leader, which means their views of what is real and important can change from moment to moment. Despite this variation on the surface, something works below – call it the 'group culture' or 'group norms' if you like, which remains relatively constant. Shortly you will be introduced to Dorrie's opening moments of the sixth session of her group. You may be able to see how Dorrie and her members react to 'information' from their own pre-existing frameworks as much as they do to information from each other.

No one is safe, not even a reader. Like Dorrie, and like the members of her group, you will most likely arrive at quite different understandings of what *is* happening, let alone what *should* happen. One reader might judge the people in this group as 'self-indulgent', and their interaction shallow and contrived. Another will experience intense fellow-feeling for one or other of the speakers. Someone else will be watching Dorrie carefully, reflecting on how soft, skilled, and caring she is. Another will be thinking: 'Well, why doesn't she get on with it?' These are just some of the infinity of understandings and reactions. Can one erect any criteria for what is 'helpful'? Let us go to Dorrie and her group to see if there are any clues.

M1: *For the last week I've been feeling very small and vulnerable. I'm all weak at the knees. I feel out of control; I want to vomit.*
M2: *I'm like that, too. I haven't a clue what's going on, and I'm desperately trying to make sense of it.*
M1: *I have these weird dreams. They're coming from a long way back. I feel like vomiting them out. I've felt like a child for the last week. Absolutely defenceless, and yet there's a freedom, too.*
M3: *It was something that Marge just said. I know it's true, but I take it as a direct attack on my way of being. Because it's such a precarious balance. My face is all hot.*

Dorrie is silent, watching the associative flow in the group. She waits for action cues – particular types of metaphors or suggestions of warm-up that indicate a move into action. While she certainly listens to each individual contribution, she also allows herself to 'hear' what is happening at levels beyond the manifest content of the group conversation. . . . What is the relationship between what this person says and what this other person says?. . . . What is not being said? Who seeks to establish a theme? Who joins in with an emerging theme? Who 'cuts across' when certain issues are raised or certain people speak? Dorrie tries to get an idea of what is going on, and to form hypotheses.

She holds these hypotheses only lightly, however. After each person speaks, Dorrie waits to see what the next person takes up – whether the hypothesis about 'what's going on' is confirmed or disconfirmed. She gives the group room to move, and avoids her own presence becoming too dominant a force in the conversation. She is alert for situations that will be most relevant to this person or to that one. It is a training group that she is running, so she tries to develop an understanding of each person so that the group time can be fully exploited on their behalf. As a psychodramatist, she is also waiting for a group theme to become clear, after which she will select the person whose story or complaint seems to represent it most completely. Dorrie has a lot to do.

In reading thus far, you might be tempted to think that this narrative is all about Dorrie and her group. The process, however, even your process of readership, is not so simple. Just as Dorrie listens for gaps, for what is taken up and what is not taken up, we too are already doing the same with her and the group. You, the reader, will already have taken in some information and have passed over other data. And I, the writer, have done the same. Not only do we make sense of the same phenomena in our different ways, but even what appear as 'phenomena' are different for us. There are some parts already in the narrative that you will not have 'read' which other readers will have spotted. And there are other parts which may be of great significance to you that others will have not seen or will have thought utterly insignificant. I am under the same restrictions;

naturally, only what I consider 'phenomena' will be reported to you, for what I do not notice I cannot even tell you about.

Back to the story: allowing this much room for further thematic material to emerge has meant that Dorrie has already passed over several promising action cues – M1 saying that she is feeling 'small and vulnerable', that she is 'weak at the knees', that she 'wants to vomit'. Any of these would have done nicely for staging as the start of a vignette or even a full drama. Should Dorrie use them?

M2 speaks as if in response to M1: he says he is 'like that, too'; that he hasn't 'a clue what's going on', and that he is 'desperately trying to make sense of it'.

In fact, M2 does not so much respond to M1 as get caught up in his own association; what he says has very little to do with what M1 says. M1 starts up again as if M2 has not spoken. Once more her imagery is vivid and concrete. Again she speaks of 'vomiting', but this time it is her 'weird dreams' that she wants to vomit. She returns to the theme of littleness and vulnerability, and adds that there is 'a freedom' in that state, too.

Dorrie still makes no intervention. Now M3 enters the conversation. Her contribution is also apparently a non sequitur to what has gone before. She speaks of an 'attack', but this attack is on her 'way of being' which she describes as in a 'precarious balance'. She too, like M1, refers to a physical state, namely, a hot face.

Since Dorrie's bent is to work extensively at the 'group process' level, she methodically notes regularities in behaviour and patterns of interaction over a period of time. She wants to find what the group norms are. Many group norms and shared beliefs are not overt or directly spoken, so Dorrie only becomes aware of them by noting what members typically do and say or what they never do and never say.

Anything remarkable yet? Even the answer to that question once again depends on your own maps, your own constructs of 'a group'. We could note that members speak in fairly colourful language, that they refer to physical concomitants of emotional states, that their statements are fairly brief, and that they concentrate on inner experiences. If you said that these were high functioning people with a fair history of groupwork behind them, you would be right: they are mostly health professionals, and are used to action methods.

Let us focus down once more on the meanings established in the group, the text that is continually being written to form the 'group story'. To interpret this text one might ask what sort of behaviours does Dorrie select and reward? What is the members' understanding of the function of the group and indeed of action methods themselves? What is permitted, what required, what forbidden? Against the group story, members will measure their own story – does it match? Are they good or bad, according to the criteria for these qualities being established? Let us go on observing carefully both sides of the interaction.

M2, whose name is Mark, responds in a way that picks up some of M3's (Melissa's) imagery – two-sidedness, or being 'torn':

M2: I'm torn between acknowledging the truth, and wanting to say 'piss off'.
D: What happens when you acknowledge the truth, Mark?
M2: Sadness. Lots of sadness.

Of all the speakers, Dorrie has responded to Mark; perhaps she is engaged by the concreteness of his being 'torn' between something and something else, both of which are named. She might well have responded to the energy of the 'piss off', but instead enquires about the other side of his dilemma. Her question 'what happens?' could be designed to glean whether he has any scenario for change in the 'outside' world; is there something promising upon which she can build? Mark's response, 'lots of sadness', actually could be a start for this process (just as anything can). But before Dorrie can go on with her questioning, Melissa speaks again, echoing Mark's dynamic of 'being torn', this time with a different content:

M3: I get torn between sitting on a response, and mouthing off – having too much to say. That's what my mother said. I say something, and there's a sea of blank faces, ten steps in front and ten behind.
D: (To Melissa) Let's have some of the group to be a sea of blank faces, ten steps in front, and ten steps behind. (This is arranged.)
M3: I want to really stand up and scream, 'Yes, I've got something'.
D: Well, do it. Do it now. (She does.)
M3: I know where it's coming from – old family stuff. Of not being heard. Of being shut up. Having arguments with my mother. She would say 'That's the end of it' and she would walk away. I'd be left standing there.
D: Choose someone from the group to be your mother. (A drama begins concerning Melissa's family-of-origin.)

In the example of dialogue and eventual psychodrama given above, M1, M2, M3, and Dorrie herself were co-creating a particular type of therapeutic reality that would be familiar to most readers of therapy texts. The difference that might strike a reader would be the action component that resulted when Dorrie suggested to Melissa that she choose some group members to be 'a sea of blank faces'. For the reader familiar with action methods, even this step would in no way be unusual. The group has established a norm of examining and expressing feelings, and relating these to family-of-origin. Note that it was Melissa who was chosen to expand the dialogue, and who was the protagonist in the eventual psychodrama. She gave a fine action cue when she mentioned the 'sea of faces' ten steps behind and in front of her; she also made a link to her mother. Perhaps both of these were irresistible to Dorrie.

Group norms

Norms can be powerful ways of ensuring that the work of the group does not get done, or that it does get done. The norm-making process is mostly unconscious, even on the leader's part: the excerpts above suggest that Dorrie and her group have built up a set of beliefs concerning why they are there in the first place, and what should be done to alleviate their difficulties. They have constructed a relationship based on the task at hand. The way in which Dorrie has warmed up the group, the things she attends to and the things she ignores, the person she or the group chooses to be protagonist, the method of action itself are all bricks in the eventual wall of group norms.

Group norms refer to the shared belief systems, the maps of reality, and the rules that groups take on. They develop right from the start – shared assumptions and mores are evident even at the first meeting, and regulate what members believe and do. Members who deviate from them can experience strong pressure to return to the fold. A norm-changer must expect to struggle as the group decides whether the new information provided by the person is syntonic or dissonant with its definition of itself.

While they are inevitable and necessary – a kind of unconscious shorthand, saving people the trouble of continually having to negotiate the rules, any group norm can become part of an enabling or restrictive group solution. They take out the element of unpredictability; people know what type of behaviour they will be criticized for, and what type of behaviour they will not. Is it all right to express anger? To be competitive? To cry? To be distant from others? To pair up with someone? The group norm will determine the 'yes' and the 'no' to these questions.

So no one bats an eye when Melissa, with Dorrie's encouragement, stands up in front of a group of people and screams 'Yes, I've got something'. She is acting within a group-attempted solution. If a member, such as Melissa, goes 'over the top' and starts shouting, that incident goes into the series of precedents – it is OK to shout. In fact, it is good. It is even better to relate one's behaviour to one's early relationship with one's mother, as M3 did. It is permissible, even rewarded, to 'regress' – to become little and needy. Intellectualization, on the other hand, may be forbidden. The knowledge of this taboo may arise by a subtle process between group members, and between group members and the leader.

In conventional group literature terms, Dorrie's group would probably be described as 'well functioning' – the members work hard at what is important to them, they utilize rather than fight against the structure planned for the group, they are high on mutual trust, they display a minimum of self-censorship and resistance, they offer mutual support yet challenge one another in a non-destructive manner, and they engage in wide-ranging exploration and sharing (Whitaker, 1985). Surely these are irreproachable as desired qualities?

The types of norms that spring up between a whole group and its leader (or a whole organization and its management, for that matter) are of particular interest to a strategic worker. They are the signposts to the well-trodden pathways within the group or organization, and concern people's attempted solutions. These solutions can lead to enjoyment and play, increase one's sense of possibility, arouse willingness to be together and to dare, and raise consciousness about important life issues. They can also leave a group 'flatter' than when it started, or randomly 'heat up' a group to no particular purpose, or teach group members boring and stale ways of psychologizing their problems and giving them a language so that they end up only being able to talk to each other.

At the end of just a few moments of Dorrie's group, the question was asked: 'Is it possible to erect any criteria for what is "helpful" in a group?' A strategic worker would say that it is not possible to determine such a thing in general; one must know the problem and why people are there. And of course one does not so much *find* why people are there – even that modest goal becomes a co-creation between leader and group members as they enter a new languaging or 'storying' domain.

Keeping one's mind on 'Why people are there' sounds easy, but in fact it tends to get a little lost in groupwork, as the community nature and exciting internal dynamics of the group take over. Most of us know from our daily experience that we cannot always get exactly what we want. Any course of action that we might take as a response to some dilemma helps us, opens us out more, or makes us more stuck, closes us down. So solutions to problems can be called 'enabling' or 'restrictive', as you will recall from the focal conflict model presented in Chapters 4 and 5. They are not enabling or restrictive absolutely, of course, but relatively so. That is, a solution that works out reasonably well for us, makes us and those around us happy, and helps us achieve our goals, is 'enabling', although it may not be perfect. One that makes us and others around us unhappy, and seems to block us in what we say we want to do, could be described as 'restrictive', even though it may not be the worst possible solution. When we are stuck, we usually go to the same restrictive solution over and over.

What does all this mean to us, who have to run groups, or consult to organizations? Naturally enough, most people do not analyse their actions in terms of attempted solutions. To do so, however, is the special province of the strategic consultant, who has the added problem of taking into account how much the *consultation itself* could become part of the client's or group's restrictive solutions. Anything that anyone does in the group – whether that person be leader or member – may lead the group to more enabling or more restrictive solutions. Interventions can bring about genuinely new solutions that lead to spontaneity, or worn-out pseudo-solutions that actually increase the problem. Though leaders apply their skills to change the group norms, even their efforts might lead to dysfunctional solutions. Enabling norms are those that allow for more trial-and-error search, and therefore spontaneity, to go on. Restrictive norms are those, generally speaking, that restrict the areas where exploration can occur.

Once again

The best warm-ups are those that evoke people's creativity and spontaneity. Sometimes these qualities come in disguise, along a path of intense pain and 'non-creativity'. This is the 'first story', often sombre, stark, and terrible. Sessions use these states as stations on the way to the 'second story', more immediate and vital. In the first story, or 'definition' of the person's life, directors help create a double description by accumulating detail, no matter how dark and terrible, and contrasting it with the second definition in surplus reality, which is usually more creative and flexible. (Please remember, though, that a 'second story' is often unnecessary if the first has been told fully – just 'laying out the system' on its own can be very helpful.) Ultimately, action methods look to the vital, active, forward-reaching roles of the group members. This view also makes sense in systemic terms: if the leader becomes too much a 'helper', members are placed in the role of 'helpless person' – a structural infelicity if ever there was one. Hence the leader's task is to warm the group up to creative aspects of themselves by means of action self-definitions, whether painful or joyous.

The purpose of systemic action methods is by now probably familiar to you: via enactment, the director maximizes the systems orientation of the members, so that new perceptions and new information may emerge. The goal, as always, is to increase the movement in the group's system, and in each member's personal system. Each member asks 'What do I need from this event?' 'What do I bring to this event?' The director asks 'What needs to be prepared?' and 'What needs to be left free?' Together they develop an 'action definition' of the system, and a new story that differs from it. They seek spontaneity at a systemic and personal level. Through their acts, through physical energy, through emotion and thinking they find (or make) a story that had not previously been available. This new information is a 'difference which makes a difference'.

What matters is a creative orientation towards one's difficulties. Hence the stage, which provides people with a space that is absolutely flexible. In contrast with the living space of 'reality', often narrow and restraining, is the stage with what Moreno calls 'its methodology of freedom'. One acts freely, as things rise up in one's mind: one creates life, whether in re-enactment of a past scene, or in something that has never happened. One acts out all those things that set us apart from others, that make us the persons we are: all those things that enable us to recognize ourselves. All those past experiences and what we learnt about them and what we felt about them; all our dreams for the future

In the theatre, one creates for the moment, not for a museum of action. 'Change', on the other hand, somehow has the element of time in it: 'difference which occurs across time is what we call "change"' (Bateson, 1972, p. 452). Change refers to the endurance of the new story. This goal of change distinguishes action methods from drama. Most groups, even most theatre groups, are pretty good at the creation of new atmospheres where 'new ideas' may come into being. But how does one get them to stay? For work with people to be called 'therapy' or 'consulting', the new interpretation of experience introduced by the director must somehow outlast the interpretation that the clients already have, but which they have found to be dysfunctional.

I have found it useful to distinguish something that is 'therapeutic' from 'therapy'. Almost anything can be therapeutic – a walk in the woods, an opera, a vacation, a good night's sleep. They are all obviously good things and certainly do us 'good'. But therapy is something different – it is designed to change our stories about ourselves. It does, or should, allow us to access spontaneity. Spontaneity in action methods usually arrives as a result of members of a social system appreciating more fully the 'what is' – their story with all its forbidden agendas. They enact the 'what is' as fully as is necessary.

Strategic consultants tend to start at a very specific level with clients – the level of the 'complaint' or problem. The problem has evolved through language on action, and is dis-solved through the same means. The consultant and group enter a new languaging system in order to generate new stories. While the specificity of their focus leads them to ask some questions of the client, which can look like the questioning of a detective trying to solve a mystery, consultants understand that they also take part in the system's process of creating language and meaning. They keep the dialogue going towards the dis-solving of the problem and the dissolving of the therapeutic system itself (Anderson and Goolishian, 1988). They ask themselves questions, too: how is this undesirable situation able to persist, and what must be done to change it?

The friendless intimate

Into a 'personal growth' group that met regularly, Di had been called in as a consultant. She asked each member what personal growth meant to them, what would be a good result if they did grow, how they would know it had happened, and why they were in the group. These are, of course, standard strategic questions about the problem that one would ask at a first interview or family session.

One woman, Marie, said that she was there because she had 'problems with intimacy'. Di enquired how she knew that she had these problems, and Marie replied that she 'found it hard to talk to people on social occasions'. Di asked her about her home life; she was married with two children. She said, on questioning, that she 'adored' her husband, and he her. She was also devoted to her two children. They were close as a family unit, went for walks together, and she was her husband's confidant, as he was hers.

None of this material had come out in the group before – such details were considered irrelevant in the 'here and now'. Intimacy, in such settings, is considered almost universally as a set of spoken exchanges concerning emotions. Di then asked Marie what her friendship circle was. She replied that it was small, because she was 'no good at intimacy'. She rarely went to the cinema with a friend or friends, she did not play cards, or do many of the 'buddy' things that friends are good for. As a result of conversing with Di, she was now able to redefine her problem as 'how to make friends, or at least a friend'.

Di asked the group what they thought Marie should do. Almost unilaterally, they advised her to express her feelings more – that way she would make friends.

The poor woman was back where she started, and would have actually had to ignore the group culture if she were to make any headway. A person whose problem with intimacy was that she is 'too good at it' is persuaded that she has 'not enough intimacy'.

Di's attitude must seem most odd to those brought up on the thicker soups of fulfilment psychology, for she tends to see Marie's problem as actually maintained by hers and the group's 'solution'. This solution – more intimacy – has a nice ring to it, looks enabling enough, but probably is not. Di investigates the requirements of the problem itself for survival (White, 1986): how is this person or group helping the problem survive? What effect does the survival of the problem have on these people? When is the problem not present – what are the exceptions?

The director wants far more than catharsis (Blatner, 1985) or a few moments of emotional release, though there is nothing wrong with either of these. The aim is new information in meaning and action. The information comes through the use of the warming-up process, the interview in role, the action phase itself, and the ritual of sharing. In all these processes, distinctions are drawn, whether verbally or in act, between one role (one way of thinking, feeling, and acting) and another. Directors know that change cannot be pushed; change comes about by working with the reactive motives, the difficulties, the restraints, the forbidden agendas.

The trigger can be a good rousing thriller, a grand epic, or the tightest and narrowest journey through personal history. Members' behaviourial, affective, perceptual, and attitudinal frameworks are activated (warmed up) and double descriptions are created. People focus on a specific area of their experience and then activate in themselves the range of roles (and the restraints on doing anything differently) that they typically invoke in such situations. In a group working on strategic principles, this specific area of experience will be closely connected with the problem that they have brought to the group in the first place. And because this is a group, rather than individual therapy or consultancy, members also warm up to each other, again engaging roles that they typically use in interaction with others. The warming-up process, therefore, is one in which members access and bring alive in themselves the way they think, feel, and act towards their problem and towards other people.

These new roles need to be functional for 'outside' living. While it is legitimate to experiment within the group context – and that might mean being a little rough or a little crazy, ultimately one looks to the person's social atom for validation of change. A strategic action group takes care that it does not become part of people's dysfunctional solutions where members attend weekly sessions in order to be 'warmed up' to difficulties, and then to have those difficulties resolved psychodramatically. Therapy can be like smoking: one has a cigarette in order to get over the craving for a cigarette, but this builds in the need for another cigarette later on.

Directors who consistently warm group members up to worrying things about their lives, or their inadequacies, may well produce groups characterized by incest and dependence, and canonize these qualities as 'therapeutic'. The members of these groups can start to believe that they are only being 'deep' or 'open' when they are acting according to group norms. This can lead to some confusion in the rest of their lives if the group ethos demands they relate to each other at the level of unhappiness, and value problem-soaked discourse above all else. Members tend to remain in such a group for a long time, believing each other to constitute a spiritual and moral elite; they may unhelpfully contrast the 'good' group with a 'bad' outside world populated by insensitive and unfeeling people.

Strategic directors foster warm-up to 'self exploration' if and when to do so serves the purpose of the member and the group. A productive group climate is one in which, amongst other things, painful experiences and mental states can be enacted in safety, and where full and unusual expression can be given to feelings that may not have been able to be experienced or expressed elsewhere. It is a climate where taboos are lifted, and spontaneity and readiness to change are encouraged. The readiness to change, however, sometimes even needs to include changes in ideas about psychodrama or therapy itself, including the recognition of when to stop. Otherwise not only do members suffer the original trauma, but become 'secondary victims' of treatment itself.

Chapter nine

Failure in warm-up

If it ain't broke, don't fix it.

Steve de Shazer

After several chapters on warm-up, you may now be getting the impression that action methods provide the answer to any difficulties in a group, and that one simply needs a mastery of warm-up techniques and sociometric procedures for a consultancy to glide along like a luxury yacht. Alas, this is not so. Groups often raise problems that call on all of a leader's proficiency, goodwill, creativity, and life experience. No one is safe from the task of being human in a group, not least the leader. To be human in itself requires spontaneity, which leaders need to develop just as much as members, or else be lost. Spontaneity is the life force, the problem solver, the spirit. No technique in this or any other book can either give it to you or take away your need for it.

Reader, you have not got this far in your profession without knowing that things can get rough in a group. A system which is in serious difficulty, grappling with profound issues about its own well-being, may simply not 'play along' with even the best designed exercises, sociometry, central concern statements, or whatever, and will apparently do everything in its power to render the consultant impotent. Desperate attempts to push the group into an 'exercise' when it is too immersed in its inner troubles will meet with failure. Even if some of the compliant members do commence the exercise, they too are likely to go to ground under withering attack from the others. The group forbidden agendas are running like bulls in the streets.

What to do? This is a chapter on failure, not success, and to a degree is exempt from that question. To be sure, there are some ways out of some difficulties, but I do not wish to make this a collection of recipes giving yet more sure-fire 'results'. You fail, and time makes things right. Or you fail, and a group member makes things right. Or you fail, and you fail.

Apologies

With the reminder that there is no substitute for spontaneity (though a little knowledge does not go astray either) let us take the simplest failure case first: the leader has mistimed something, or has forgotten something, or is involved in disputes with the group because he or she is simply wrong. When an error is clearly the leader's, it is best to say so immediately, and pass on. Nothing is lost by this – indeed much can be gained from the leader's adopting a simple, human, and dignified stance of error. It is a straightforward matter, surely.

Unfortunately, events in a group are often not simple enough for even that solution to be given as a recipe. One has to consider the recursiveness operating in any human system: in a group, a mistake may not simply be one's 'own'. This statement in no way implies that group leaders are never incompetent, heavy-handed, and owing an apology to everyone. Far from it. But leaders need to take care that they do not burden the group with unprofitable apologies and force the group to work through the leader's own 'material' – their own tendency to be guilty or responsible when chaos or deadness takes over. Every moment that the group members are in the group is a moment when the task of the group can be done. If the leader does feel guilty and incompetent, it may be preferable to use the incident (or lack of incident, if the trouble is that the group is in the doldrums) in the best way one can, and to refer the matter later to one's supervisor.

Take the case of a director having in fact been leading the group reasonably competently – that is, when a simple apology for things going wrong is not in order. Indeed such an apology may actually prevent members from gaining something valuable from the experience of stuckness, conflict, or poor warm-up. Directors can start to explore what the conflict has meant for individuals, for different sub-groups and for the group at large. For example, members can be asked what it would mean for them if they *did* do the exercise, what it would mean if the director *were* mistaken, what they have done in their domestic lives at other times when they *are* stuck, and other standard procedures for making everything that happens in the group grist for the spontaneity mill. It is clear that unwarranted apologies would cut short the opportunities that these questions raise, and cheat members of their chance to explore back-home correlates of this stuckness, challenge, or boredom. On the one hand, then, it is incorrect for directors to be poker-faced, never-wrong, omnipotent figures, and on the other, they act in an unsound fashion if they give themselves over to inappropriate apology.

Once again, care should be taken that a moralistic stance is not adopted, and that an examination of the 'resistance' is truly on the members' side, rather than in the director's defence. The director can ask questions such as:

When things are wrong and you go flat, what stops you from pulling yourself out of the hole? . . . Put a chair over there for the thing that stops you. Address the chair 'You who stop me'.

The above example illustrates only one of the ways by which directors feel their way back into what is happening in the group, so that it can make progress. The group, of course, does not make progress only when things are going well, but also in adversity, by working through painful conflicts, aridity, and misunderstanding. When spontaneity is lost, it is important to note the differences between members' spontaneity state and their current state: 'What is it like for you when you feel indecisive and confused?' 'What was it like when you felt you knew exactly what to do?. . . . What is the difference?' 'What does it mean to you now to realize that difference?' . . . are questions that directors can ask. They can also express surprise that the group is doing as well as it is doing given its difficulties, and ask members to account for why it has taken them this long to break down.

Sometimes the warm-up failure has to do with the director's misreading of the group central concern, or by the group not seeming to have an identifiable central concern in the first place. This would suggest either lack of customership on the part of members, or bungling by the director, or both. In a group, of course, members can have overall customership, but be listless or out of sorts on a particular day. There is no need, and it is not possible, to make every post a winner. Directors can effectively act in several ways:

(1) By restating the central concern as they saw it, and asking for an action sociogram as to how warmed up people are to that issue (for instance on a line from 1 to 100, or by placing the concern – represented by a cushion – in the centre and having people locate themselves at various radii from the centre).

(2) By the simplest of conversational methods, for example by just asking members 'what's going on for you . . . for you . . . for you', and linking the answers a little, without being too clever and showy about it.

(3) By asking for a metaphor for the group in its present state, and basing the action on the one that makes one's heart race a little.

(4) By asking for the title of a group play, as if the group is being scripted

by a playwright. The 'plot' can then be evoked and acted out. One can do this quite economically, spending a mere 15 minutes or so, and then leading back to what they are all there for (though the play itself will probably contain this, if only one has the wit to look).

(5) By taking the new central concern, which may be anger at the director for 'failing' them, or apathy, or resentment, and beginning the warming-up process afresh with a revised statement.

(6) By 'sweating it out'. Life is not perfect, and nor will be the functioning of persons who have come together because of some difficulty or other (not to mention the poor leader, and his or her own forbidden agendas leading them to this branch of psychological practice).

Failure in individual warm-up

Customership

Let us now consider some situations where an individual, rather than the whole group, manifests disquiet. This disquiet seems at odds with the mainstream sentiment. Members can be at odds because they are not warmed up enough, or because they are 'too' warmed up. In either case, directors need to have their wits about them. When an individual is not warmed up 'enough', and the director has appropriately employed the techniques and skills available in the group, it is a fair sign that the person iş not a 'customer' for change, though he or she may profit in a general way from being in the group.

In the extract below, Mandy espouses one of the most revered norms of a personal growth group based on action methods – that of spontaneity itself. The director, Di, is inquiring what Mandy wants out of the group:

M: I want to become more spontaneous and direct.
D: How is not being spontaneous and direct a problem?

The last thing that Mandy thinks she will be asked is to examine her desire to be spontaneous. Yet her very search for 'spontaneity' may be the problematic behaviour that prevents her from interactions that are pleasurable and life-enhancing. In questioning the desire for spontaneity, Di is behaving unusually in terms of anticipated norms of fulfilment psychology. She would be expected to take Mandy's statement as one that represents a real problem – as indeed it may do. That is precisely why, in the role of naive enquirer, she asks how not being spontaneous is a problem. She has to stay clear not only of the more obviously restrictive solutions put up by the members, but also of the more subtle ones put up by the therapeutic culture itself. Avoiding these latter presents far more of a challenge.

She asks simple questions about the status of the problem, rather than instantly joining Mandy's (and the group's) map of reality, which might be that 'lack of spontaneity' is the worst fate that can befall anybody, and that to 'have' spontaneity will be the solution to all one's problems. Spontaneity is construed as a 'thing' rather than a set of interactions appropriate for given circumstances, an 'it' that one can 'have'.

D: *How long has your lack of spontaneity been a bother to you?*
M: *Oh, for quite a while, really.*
D: *Has it changed at all – any times you've felt more or less spontaneous?*
M: *Oh, the last few months, maybe less. It's a bit hard to say.*
D: *So that would take us into late last year, I suppose.*
M: *I'm not sure.*
D: *Were the leaves on the trees when you began to think you were not spontaneous? What was happening for you then?*
M: *I don't think I was ever spontaneous.*

The 'how long?' is a typical strategic question, and is also helpful from a dramatic point of view, since it can serve to prompt a particular scene amenable for staging. Di invites Mandy to warm up to action by taking 'a few months' literally, and asking her for a more specific time when 'not being spontaneous' began to be perceived as a greater problem in comparison with some other time. Notice that she does not buy into Mandy's assumption that 'lack of spontaneity' is a problem in itself. She figures that if she joins Mandy's story, which says she is not spontaneous, she may 'canonize' dysfunctional solutions in Mandy herself and in the group.

The demands for theatre work to be crisp and elegant and the demands of strategic therapy not to contribute to dysfunctional maps of reality are at this stage merging. If reasonable aesthetic and interactive norms are broken in a group, the living contact between therapist and group members can be lost. This is nowhere more true than in a group that has formed itself around action methods. If Di tries to 'make' Mandy spontaneous, she is likely to join Mandy's own depressed system, and they both will fail.

D: *What would you do differently if you were more spontaneous and direct?*
M: *I wouldn't be so fearful of the consequences. If a response pops up, which it does incredibly quickly . . . just have the response, and then just take what comes.*
D: *How often would you have to do this to know that you were*

successful at it. What would be an acceptable difference between you now and you then?

M: *I think . . . Um, I think . . . taking a risk of being talkative, having too much to say. I have no picture of how it would be.*

D: *What would be a little change – one that you would at least know that you were on the way. Don't picture how you would do it; just one little change so that you would know when this was less of a problem.*

M: *Oh, that's really hard.*

This person is not warmed up, and is not a customer for change at the moment. Because Mandy is not really a customer, there is little point in the director using her skills to warm her up, as the result will not only be no change, but could be even worse – a further entrenchment of dysfunctional solutions around the issue of 'spontaneity'. What is lacking most of all is a sense of conviction that would normally manifest itself in some specificity. Mandy has done nothing 'wrong' by wanting to work on spontaneity, but the director would do her or the group no favour if she were to agree on this as a contract. The result would be neither aesthetic nor pragmatic. Di's best course may be to compliment Mandy on her desire to expand herself (disturbing motive), recognize in her own language some of the restrictions facing her at the moment (reactive motive), and join her empathically at her current solution. Mandy returns to the group circle. After a while, and with occasional attention from Di to her current dialectic, Mandy may warm up to customership.

The survival of a problem – exercises

Mandy's searches for 'spontaneity' as an abstract quality in itself may be an habitual and failed solution. It is a *prerequisite* – something that she thinks she must have before she can have something else: 'If I am spontaneous, *then* I will be able to . . . .' Sometimes the prerequisites themselves do us in. 'If I weren't so shy, then I would be able to meet women'; 'If I could only get my anger out, then I would be peaceful'; 'If I didn't have this anxiety about directing, then I could be a great director'. In strategic terms, it is often a mistake to accept and then 'work on' the prerequisite – that is, to have lengthy interactions about shyness, getting the anger out, or directorial anxiety. The resulting drama will tend to lack earthiness.

The therapeutic maxim that one has to feel differently before one can behave differently is not borne out in real life, and nor need it be in therapeutic life. Presuppositions, including our presuppositions about therapy itself, are only maps. Action can precede feeling; feeling can catch up later. So can 'understanding'. If Milton Erikson made any contribution to therapy, it was this.

When clients are asked what they want to *do* differently, they often launch into a description of presumed underlying matters, presenting them as the 'real problem'. They do this in good faith, of course, and in order to be helpful, but their explanation itself is often part of the restrictive story that they are telling; does this sound familiar to those of you who are group leaders? The manner in which the problem is typically described is in itself oppressive. The very languaging, the storying itself constitutes the problem, and subjugates the person. Here are some exercises for a training group that may help with the problem of how to devise a story that outlasts the old story, and is not so destructive.

In pairs, interview the other person as if for a drama. Develop a common understanding of what is going to happen in the drama. The understanding should usually end up in a simple statement.

Work out between you how much progress towards the goal the 'client' would construe as success.

Get the 'client' to stand on a line 'from 0 to 100%' which expresses where they are now with respect to their problem, and where they would be if they knew that they were making some progress.

Asking what one's minimal goal might be – what would indicate some success in the therapy or consultancy – is helpful. This way of contracting alerts clients from the outset to noticing change, and can later be a lever for change. In fact, the smaller 'percentage of improvement' that the clients agree to, the better, for two reasons. The first is that the therapy is less likely to be put in the position of 'failing', of being yet another disappointment. If therapists can persuade clients to go for minimum 'percentage' success, it is very likely that they will achieve at least that measure of success.

'One per cent' of change is usually quite actionable, and so for that matter is '10 per cent'. Problems start when clients want new personalities or new situations entirely. Reaching for 'a complete change' might well be part of the client's idealizing system which is contributing to their unhappiness in the first place. Depressed people might idealize themselves as exuberant, fit, garrulous, and magnetic. Bulimics might idealize themselves as fashionable, gaunt, and desirable. When the image breaks down, they binge on tablets, cigarettes, or food. Then the guilt starts, followed by more idealization, followed by more bust/remorse.

The second reason for arguing for small changes is that in persuading clients to go for a minimum of change, the therapist is already working dialectically by taking the opposite pole to the change pole (or the 'reactive motive' in Whitaker's (1985) terminology). The client then takes the radical, more hopeful stance of anticipating at least *some* change. This sort of change in fact *is* likely to happen, and the therapeutic task then becomes to help people notice it. The very noticing of it, of course, expands the change (see section on 'Responding to responses'). It helps clients out of their stuckness between the disturbing motive (desire for comfort, love, etc.) and the reactive motive (usually fear that these desires will be punished) the result of which is a highly restrictive and stuck solution (depression; binge).

Consultants can also have another target, apart from homing in so directly on the experience of the problem for the individual. This target is how the problem is interpersonally maintained. What does the problem need for its survival? In other words, one now moves to a *systemic* enquiry by finding out who else is involved? The effects in a social atom of the person changing are highly relevant when a person is considering doing something differently.

1. In pairs, take a problem and set out the likely social atom around that problem. What does that problem need for its survival? What do the people have to tell themselves, and what do they have to do so that problem can go on?
2. Now work the other way round. One person (A) tell the other (B) of a social atom that they know. Now get B to set out the likely problems that come from that social atom. When you have finished, check with A to see how right and how wrong you are.

People do not usually have much luck with their predictions in the second exercise. Is this because they are just amateurs? Possibly not. In human affairs, we tend to think that problems come about only from hatred and neglect. Strategic therapists take a softer line: we betray ourselves and others by forbidden agendas involving love and loyalty as much as by greed, selfishness, and malice. This is where the first exercise comes in: it is very hard for a person to change if they are undertaking their present behaviour out of love and loyalty to someone else. A young woman, for example, might not be able to lose weight, no matter how hard she tries, if the forbidden agenda is that she does not want to become a rival to her mother for her father's attentions. She is 'restrained' from doing anything else than putting on more weight until these agendas are revealed. One often does not know the source of one's own restraints. A person may be restrained from being more assertive, for example, because it might cut across their idea of being a loving person.

In the following dialogue, the director undertakes a brief systemic investigation prior to action work. The investigation is not being represented here as comprehensive – merely as a 'starter' to gain an idea of what may be going on in the social atom that would restrain a person from believing that they had rights.

Mort, so you want to be more assertive with people. . . . What people do you have in mind? Mmmm. . . . And how are you not being assertive with them now. Show us, here, in action, you not being assertive with this person.
(Mort does so, using an auxiliary.)
OK. Now this question might seem a bit strange, Mort, but how would you say not being assertive is a problem to you?
OK, I see: it especially affects your relationship with your friend, Billy, does it? Now, have you ever been what you would call assertive with Billy? You have? Let's see you act that time.
Good, now who apart from yourself and Billy would be most affected if you became more assertive with him? Your girlfriend, eh?
Choose someone from the group to be her, and let's see what goes on when you act in this new way towards Billy.

One can be meticulous *and* tender. The inquiries in the imaginary case above have been 'packed in' for the sake of rapid illustration. In the 'real life' context of a group, though, the questions should not inhibit the warm-up, need not all be asked, and certainly need not be asked one after the other in the way that I have illustrated. Their sociometric ramifications can easily be portrayed in the drama itself, embedded in action. It is the fact of having an epistemology around the problem, rather than a personality theory or a theory of psychopathology, that distinguishes strategic work from more traditional psychologies. The drama and the action work can be as voluptuous as you like, provided the framework of the problem and its attempted solution is there.

An exercise that trainees love now follows. It is based on Strong's (1968) interpersonal influence theory, in which he maintains that one person will tend to influence another if they are perceived as competent, attractive, and trustworthy. Part two of the exercise – of establishing whether the person has worked in this area before and what the results have been – is included because it is part of the strategic repertoire, and also because the very investigation of that question tends to make the 'client' feel that the questioner is indeed competent and trustworthy.

(1) In pairs, establish a relationship where the other person feels comfortable with you (not just feelings, but also thoughts that you are competent to direct).

(2) Establish whether this person has worked in the area before. Find out what has succeeded and what has failed in the previous work.

(3) Enjoy yourself. Feel likeable. Feel the pleasure of doing this work. After all, you are doing what you have been waiting and paying and studying a long time to do.

Focusing on change, the strategic method attempts to help clients or group members to recognize when things are different. It tries to get people's solutions from being relatively restrictive to relatively enabling. It examines the status of the problem, the co-evolution of the problem, and any alliances and coalitions in the group around the problem. It takes as its premise that current interactions between the group member and involved others, either inside or outside the group, are central in shaping and maintaining the problem behaviour.

Monopolization, vulnerability, and overheated warm-up

In the early hours of a group, one person often seems to 'monopolize' the group's time, apparently wishing to be in control or to gain everyone's attention. Although at first the time-grabbing behaviour seems to be a matter of individual personality, further reflection may suggest a more systemic foundation. For example, Miranda's talking a great deal at the beginning of a group may be part of a restrictive solution on the part of all members, at least in that they do not try to stop her. The solution for them, therefore, may be: 'If Miranda talks, we do not have to.' The director does not need to focus so much on Miranda, but on the group's adoption of the restrictive solution, and they might be challenged on the issue.

Whether the director worked with Miranda or with the whole group, a useful conceptual framework, once again, is that of focal conflict – 'if this behaviour represents a solution, what is the disturbing motive and what is the reactive motive for a) Miranda, and b) the group members?' The disturbing motive for all of them might well be safety – Miranda talks endlessly and the group does nothing about it because they are frightened. They may be frightened of Miranda herself, or frightened of what could happen if she *stops* speaking. Miranda may not wish so much to 'dominate' the situation as to quell intolerable anxiety about being in the group in the first place.

Sometimes a member seems not so much frightening as acutely vulnerable. The vulnerability of one member tends to act as a brake on the behaviour of the others. Suppose his name is Mick. . . . No one dares interact with Mick for fear of doing more damage, or for imagined guilt about the damage they have already done. Whitaker (1985, pp. 325–327) conducts an excellent discussion on this matter: she suggests that some persons so regarded are not as vulnerable as other members think, but are defined as vulnerable partly because of how they present themselves and partly because others maintain fantasies of their own destructive powers.

A declaration or appearance of personal weakness can turn the 'weak' person into a very powerful figure in the group. Once again systems thinking is called for: Mick may present himself as vulnerable 'in order' to cue others to respond to him in particular ways. If the leader co-operates with the fantasies of power and destruction sometimes swirling around a vulnerable person, such fantasies will continue untested in the group. But if, once again following a focal conflict model, the leader sees both Mick and the group's behaviour in terms of restrictive solutions, they can explore the topic dynamically yet safely: 'You want to help yourselves and Mick, and put a stop to what he's doing; but on the other hand, you fear that he will fall to pieces if you confront him in any way; therefore you pretend that nothing is happening at all.'

In issues of power/powerlessness, fragility/stability, topdog/underdog, etc., it is helpful once again to remember that these are stories or descriptions. The first step is to notice out loud what the story or description is: to face a situation (monopolization, extreme vulnerability) rather than pretend that it does not exist. Then it is a good idea to sort out which feelings belong to whom (especially around the issue of vulnerability), and to display confidence that the group can deal with all the difficulties implied by the first description, and with whatever difficulties might arise if a new description were to be entertained. Finally, directors need not accept responsibility for problems that properly belong to the group as a whole and which they could not manage single-handedly even if they wanted to.

Another type of difficulty occurs when an individual seems over warmed up, and the rest of the group is not with him or her. One tries simply to 'ignore' such individuals to one's cost, since their tormented and restless presence in the group can place great pressure on the leader and other members. On the other hand, the fact that someone is highly warmed up and 'bursting' to do an individual vignette or psychodrama by no means indicates that this is what should happen. It would almost certainly be inappropriate, for example, in a group that has met for curriculum planning. It may not even be indicated in a 'personal growth' group, for reasons that I have suggested before: it is too early; the central concern of the group has not been clarified, or it is inappropriate to have a single protagonist because it will tend to 'freeze' other people from becoming actors.

An individual's apparently personal and idiosyncratic warm-up needs to be related to the group in at least two ways: in terms of personal connection with others, so that the person is 'linked up', and in terms of understanding the phenomenon so that the group, the director, and the person involved have new information upon which to base action.

At the first session of a group which has met for training purposes, Matt announces that he is feeling panicky, detached, and 'cloudy', and that he has no idea why he is feeling this way. No one else in the group has made a similar announcement. The director has the option of

(a) Doing 'personal' work with Matt on his feeling of panic, such as asking him to choose someone to be the cloud, reversing roles with it, and getting the cloud to tell Matt what it is 'protecting' him from. What it is stopping him from seeing, etc.

(b) Getting a couple of people to support Matt and then moving on.

(c) Working sociometrically: 'Who else in the group feels like Matt?' OR 'Matt, as you speak, who in the group do you feel best understands you? Towards whom do you feel closest at the moment?'

(d) Working with strategic sociometry (see full chapter): 'Maude, when Matt speaks about how upset he is at the moment, who do you think listens with greatest interest? Who would most notice if Matt stopped feeling upset? Max, if Matt were not upset now, who do you think would be? Mary, do you think Matt will become more upset or less as the group moves on? Who gets most upset in the group so far when Matt gets upset?'

There are virtually no limits to the sorts of moves that can be made in order to present Matt's distress in its possible systemic basis. Some of the most useful actions are based on an hypothesis about the system, rather than simply about Matt. Sometimes, of course, one has not even the inklings of an hypothesis, and must enquire, or simply wait, until an hypothesis suggests itself. Then one needs more questions, or an enactment itself, to test the hypothesis. Whatever happens, Matt's upsetness needs to be seen in the light of his doing his best as he sees it. His distress may also be evaluated in terms of his trying to do a service of some sort for himself or for the group: maybe to save it from peril, maybe to become the 'patient' of the group to distract it and keep it from disintegrating.

If something positive happens during the investigation itself, the director can draw attention to the new description: 'What happened just then?' 'What was it like for you to feel that spark of life?' etc. Differences in a 'negative' direction – towards flattened affect, depression, confusion, strictness, rigidity, uncreativity, etc. – are as valuable to point out as differences in a positive direction. Although both protagonist and director are quite naturally biased in favour of differences that are positive, pointing out negative changes or deeper stuckness and contrasting them with more desirable states is another way of getting the two stories about oneself on to the cutting room floor.

Just as directors can alert individuals to notice differences in their behaviour, they can also draw a group's attention to those differences. For this reason, it is desirable that directors keep some sort of mental record of the group's central concerns as they arise. This is important on two levels: firstly, as the central concern is tied in with the contract that each individual member has made in coming to it, a statement about changes in the central concern becomes a statement of how each individual member is getting on with their contract. Pointing up the *differences* in the central concern as the group goes forward is similar to alerting individuals to progress – to moving from one kind of narrative to another. Drawing the group's attention to changes in the central concern over time can be even more powerful than drawing an individual's attention to such changes, for reasons stated elsewhere.

'Resistance'

Focal conflict-based warm-ups are particularly suited to group members who operate on 'defiance-based' cognitive styles. To defy the part of the message that restrains them from changing, or relaxing, or entering fully into the group, they must change, relax, or enter. The desired response is not for them to do any one thing in particular, but to reflect on their accustomed ways of handling the situation – that is, their 'solution'. Ideally, a dialectical intervention aims at changing systemic premises affecting the members' behaviour. The question can be asked indirectly:

Milton, what is an aspect of Marge's behaviour that she would like to rule out? What is an aspect of the group that she would like to destroy?

Focal conflict interventions imply that the present behaviour regarded as a 'resistance' is redefined dialectically – that is, the positive intention behind the behaviour is included in the definition of the behaviour. This so-called resistance (the reactive motive strongly operating to provide restrictive solutions) can genuinely be seen as a part of a person or system that looks after stability. It regards the present situation (the solution), although perhaps not perfect, as preferable to the risks involved in taking on a new situation.

'Resistance' is present in most things we do – lying on a beach, we think perhaps we should be working, or at least be more creative; getting married, there is at least a little pocket of resistance – maybe we should not be getting married at all, or not be marrying this person; when working, we often wish we were lying on a beach. So when it comes to attending a workshop, a seminar, or therapy group, one might expect quite substantial 'resistance' to several people or factors: to the leader; to being there at all rather than doing something else; to changing one's ways; to meeting new people; to doing activities which most people would regard as odd. Milton Erikson used to say that if the therapist did not put in the 'not', the client would. There is a big 'No' in us all, ready to be activated at the start of something new, especially something that promises to upset our equilibrium. The fact that we might be paying to have our equilibrium upset seems to matter not one whit.

Chapter ten

Classical sociometry

'Know thyself,' said the ancient Greeks. 'Know thy neighbour,' say the more practical Americans.

P. J. O'Rourke

Where do you stand?

People are unendingly curious about where they stand with others: workers like to know how they are doing with the boss and other colleagues; family members speculate on (or know only too well) their position according to closeness to mother, closeness to father, most sensitive, most courageous, and so on. It does not stop with oneself: ever concerned with pecking orders, hierarchies, and alliances, people also like to know about others' relationships and standing with each other, even when they themselves are not directly involved. In fact, most gossip is about such matters: who is choosing whom, who is above whom, who agrees with this person and disagrees with that person. Even people who 'never gossip' seem to have quite an informed idea of hierarchies and choices; if pressed, they can usually guess at their own position, and the position of others with others. In all these instances, they act informally as sociometrists.

Formal sociometry attempts to put some structure on this process; a sociometric test investigates the choice activity of a group, yielding information about the life of social systems. Sociometry means 'companion measure'. Moreno designed it as a measure, a 'new science', though its ultimate purpose was transcendence, not science. In the act of choice, one lays one's being on the line, as it were. It was a way to achieve the potential that he saw in all human groups to love, share, and face their truth. He wanted people to be aroused 'to act, to choose, to reject' (1953, p. 122), by active and public choosing. By making choices overt and energetic, Moreno hoped that individuals would be more spontaneous, and organizations and group structures would become fresh, clear, and lively.

Sociometric explorations lay bare the hidden structures that give a group its form: the alliances, the hidden beliefs, the forbidden agendas, the ideological agreements, the 'stars' of the show, positive and negative. Sociometry focuses on the connections which exist between group members, and the reasons for those connections. But despite its concern with connections, it is not in itself necessarily an 'encounter'; it is a measure, an information-provider that stresses the social nature of everything we are and do. Our actions, beliefs, and feelings come from, and are maintained by the actions, beliefs, and feelings of others.

> The basis of sociometric classification is not a psyche which is bound up with the individual's organism but individual organisms moving around in space in relation to other things or other organisms also moving around them in space.
>
> (Moreno, 1953, p. 178)

The sociometric measures do not have to be overt: effective directors mentally assess sociometry during all stages of psychodramatic work: at the time of warm-up, during the enactment, and especially during the sharing. These covert assessments of where group members stand with each other differ in extent and intensity from formal sociometric tests, which may run from elaborate pen-and-paper affairs, to simple action choices based on a single criterion. The essence of sociometry, though, is that people are placed 'nearer or further away' from others on the basis of what is called a 'criterion'.

Two types of criterion

No doubt 'criterion' and 'choice' are the most important concepts in sociometry. A sociometric criterion is the point over which people are asked to measure their similarities and differences. It is usually expressed as a choice: 'With whom would you most like to. . .?' This sort of choice can imply two kinds of actions, according to how the criterion is formulated. The first way leads to the identification of a set of sociometric 'stars' – that is, people in the group who embody the fantasies of the members on a certain dimension – 'beauty', say, or 'vitality' or 'courage'. Here are a few examples: starting with the instruction 'Put your hand on the shoulder of . . .' the director can choose a number of criteria:

1. A person with whom you would want to share something exquisite in nature.
2. A person with whom you would want to share something exquisite that is made by human beings – a painting, perhaps, or a building.
3. Someone that you could feel very sad with, and get support – not 'help', just support.

4. Someone that it would be good to go berserk with in a thunderstorm.
5. Someone who would give you good advice on personal matters.
6. Someone who would help you with a project.
7. Someone whom you could tell your feelings to, even if it meant confrontation.
8. Someone that you would like to be on your knees with, a fag hanging out of your mouth, scrubbing floors.

When directors use sequential criteria rapidly to connect two disparate concepts ('give support/go berserk in a thunderstorm') or to suggest a criterion that in itself creates surprise ('on your knees, a fag hanging out of your mouth'), members' rigid thinking tends to break up. Furthermore, the spread of 'stars' that develops from each criterion demonstrates the multiple role requirements and role fulfilments in a group. This procedure ensures that all members are included as potential 'stars', depending on the criterion.

Working quickly and diversely also develops a genuine sociometric consciousness; the group starts to understand itself as an ecology. Groups are systems that rapidly, but sometimes rigidly, become complete in themselves with their own gatekeepers, Virgin Marys, managers, doormats, sluts, accountants, heroes, rakes, devils, secretaries, explorers, wimps, and other functionaries. This is all very well, and only need be disturbed if the role requirements become dysfunctional or rigid. In such cases, it is as if the members are unable to take any role in the group except those that they have assigned to themselves or to which they have been assigned by some unspoken and mysterious process.

A second sort of sociometric criterion does not look for stars, but merely seeks to divide the group according to some state or preference. Examples of these types of criteria are: 'Stand up this end of the room if you are very familiar with the notions of sociometry, and stand at the other end if all this is completely new to you'. . . . Or, 'Stand here (gestures) if you want a break at 3.30, and here (moves to other side of room) if you want to work right through'.

In this second type of criterion, no 'stars' emerge, because things, rather than persons, are being decided upon – familiarity with a process, or preference for breaks, in the examples. Such criteria are usually referred to as 'Diagnostic', because they give the leader and group an analysis of the state of the group. Star criteria are the most common variety, and we will use them for most of our definitions at this early stage. They can be posed at a general level, such as: 'With whom in the group would you like to spend a day?' or can be made more specific, such as: 'With whom in the group would you like to spend a day shopping for shoes?'

Usually, the people chosen will be different in each case. The more specific the criterion, the more information each person has on which to base his or her choice. Hale (1974) lists other criteria, such as actual versus hypothetical criteria. Actual criteria concern situations that have a fair likelihood of eventuating, such as

With whom in the group would you like to have lunch today? (Actual-star)

With whom do you feel most intimate in the group? (Actual-star)

Stand on a line from 1 to 100 as to how much you would like to go for a walk. (Actual-state)

Stand this end of the room if you feel the group is very intimate this afternoon, and down this end if you feel it lacks intimacy. (Actual-state)

Hypothetical criteria, on the other hand, concern more remote or speculative possibilities, such as questions about who a person would choose to take on a long ocean voyage, or, if each member had been born of the opposite sex, who in the group would they most resemble. Hypothetical criteria can lead to fun and action, as in the following example which elicits members' preference for taking up certain roles:

If you were reincarnated and the choices were a fish (sets out chair), a bird (sets out chair), a dog (sets out chair), or a horse (chair), which would you choose? Stand nearest to one of those chairs.

If you were reincarnated as a man (chair), or woman (chair), which would you like to be? OR

This end of the room represents red, and this end the colour blue; stand at one or other end according to which colour you are at the moment.

Whether criteria are hypothetical or actual, it is well for group leaders to chose criteria that establish a vibrant sense of the group, and clarify pathways for activity. For example:

Go and stand next to the person with whom you would wish to work on this afternoon's exercise. (Star)

Put your hand on the shoulder of a person in the group that you do not know very well, but would like to know better. (Star)

Stand up this end if you want a psychodrama session this morning, and up this end if you want a teaching session. (State)

One of the liveliest uses of sociometry comes as a result of something that is actually happening. Let us say a group member, Mary, says that she is feeling 'anxious' on that day, and others relate strongly to that statement. 'Anxiety' may become the theme and central concern of the group, and members can then be asked to place themselves in relation to Mary's anxiety. In this instance, they are not 'choosing' Mary for anything, and nor has the director given Mary's anxiety a value – members merely group themselves around her and past her according to their assessment of her state and their own. But they are now actors, committing themselves 'on the line' by deed, and thereby the room becomes lively, dramatic, tense.

Various forms of sub-groupings can be revealed by a sociometric test. Where people frequently cluster together, no matter what the criterion question, a sub-group whose criteria for membership are deep within the role structures of its individual members may be said to have formed. Sub-group members consistently either choose one of their members as sociometric star, or else they will all choose a person who is not one of their members. They generally have one mind on any issue, and tend to share or act out the same solutions to personal or group dilemmas (see *isolated dyad* on page 133). How they communicate their decisions to one another is often mysterious. Perhaps they talk with each other so often outside group time that they have pre-formed opinions on most topics. Perhaps the connection is stronger and more esoteric.

Sociometry does not always need to be enacted in the same way. Any process involving information about differences and similarities can be regarded as 'sociometric'. Participants can respond verbally to criterion questions, or write their answers in a sort of map of the group, or tell their partners, or use the more usual actions such as going over to the nominated person and putting a hand on their shoulder, or position themselves on an imaginary scale of 0 to 100. Later, some sociometric procedures to be done in pairs or fours will be suggested.

Star sociometries

At any given time, people naturally relate more strongly to some group members than to others. Why it is this person now, and that person at some other time, is more mysterious; maybe certain people embody a 'group theme' at a particular stage. Such reasoning is almost part of a sacred text in group therapy literature, and it does have a certain validity even though at shop-floor level one's motives may be far less grand: this person is attractive, this one was nice to me as we walked in, and so on. Let me not be too zealous in my attempts to demystify the sometimes irritating pseudo-mysticism that goes on in groups – often at the expense of the truly mysterious and holy. Attractiveness and niceness will in fact usually connect to a group theme – they will be greedily sought specials on some days, and go unnoticed on others, if anger, say, is on the menu.

The thematic process, therefore, is not entirely random. Emotions and themes that typically preoccupy a group are courage, vitality, attractiveness, suffering, sexuality, expressiveness, intimacy, and anger; some members will embody these themes in the group fantasy at any given time. On a world scale, Elvis Presley, Francis of Assisi, Colonel Gadaffi, or Marilyn Monroe might be regarded as sociometric stars, each capturing different sorts of choices for different cultures and different eras. On both the local and the world scale, as the culture of the group or world changes, so will the sociometric stars. If Marilyn Monroe were starting her career now, she might have more difficulty in becoming a star, or she might find it easier, depending on how she embodied certain cultural values. Her stardom in the fifties was no doubt partly a product of the Hollywood publicity machine, but at the same time that machine was also reactive to popular taste in a mutual influence process. The star is a star for the time, and not necessarily for all time. Similarly, a group member at one stage embodies the fantasies of the group, and at another does not, partly because those fantasies are themselves changing. The group moves on in its concerns, and the former star no longer twinkles so brightly, and a new person becomes the ideal.

Stardom moves around according both to group culture and to the diverse criteria suggested: for example, 'psychotelic stars' are highly chosen for personal attributes and subjective feelings, and will not necessarily be the same ones as the 'sociotelic stars', who are highly chosen for their skills and intelligence. Sociotelic stars tend to be the people in the group who can get the video equipment to work or who know the telephone number of the taxi company. They are often despised in a group fixated on intimacy needs; such fixation, however, may be more indicative of stuck thinking on the part of group members, and even the underrated individuals themselves, than of appropriate therapeutic norms. Sociotelic stars are able to further the work of the group as well as anyone else, provided their contribution can be recognized and not disqualified by a psychotelic maniac of a director.

Since reality is many-sided, measures of the reality of a group need also to be many-sided. The group needs to be seen from several angles, so that its 'true' reality may be appreciated by means of information about difference. Directors wishing to broaden the sociometric consciousness of the group, therefore, need to vary the criteria upon which sociometric choices are made. By asking different sorts of criterion questions, they are effectively issuing embedded commands to the group to think along different lines. In effect, this process disturbs the culture of the group, breaks its rigid thinking, and allows it to develop new patterns of thought and interaction. If the group has settled on one set of stars representing intimacy dimensions (psychotelic stars) and then are asked to choose on another kind of dimension altogether, say, that of practical skills, not only is there a greater awareness of the spread of talent and roles within the group, but the group is refocused from its obsession with one type of role constellation, and, by implication, one type of 'cure' for itself.

Scapegoating and isolation

If, upon the instruction 'Put your hand on the shoulder of the person here with whom you have conflict', nearly everyone puts their hand on one person's shoulder, a group *scapegoat* may be revealed. If the instruction is varied on a second round to: 'Put your hand on the shoulder of the *next* person with whom you have conflict', and no one is able to do it, the leader can be fairly sure that something strange is happening in the group. Everyone has conflict with just one person – otherwise everything is perfect! Perhaps that person is displacing much of the other conflict that may otherwise be happening. Perhaps they are a sort of lightning conductor in the group.

Reciprocity is a very important factor in the choice of a negative or positive sociometric star. Consider these three positions: a star who is highly chosen and who reciprocates those choices has a solid base for interaction and support in the group; a highly chosen person who does not reciprocate has a less secure position; the *star of incongruity* has the highest number of unreciprocated relationships, and is in fact likely to be a focus in the group due to the stress resulting from being the unchosen chooser. The group members find such people puzzling, and the unchosen choosers in turn find the other members puzzling.

There is a fourth position: the *isolate* does not choose and is not chosen. Isolated people suffer greatly, and this suffering can cause the other group members to feel uncomfortable and often guilty. Isolates' influence in a group can be deathly, to the extent that they can bring about its dissolution when other members are not able to cope with their own feelings about another person being isolated. An *isolated dyad* is a pair who choose only each other – they too can affect the identity of the group and distract it from its task. Members will tend to feel judged by such a dyad, certain that the pair is sharing secrets and commenting on their fellows. The apparent closeness of the dyad is inviting, but at the same time the members-at-large feel a certain contempt and anger about the pairing. Thus a dyad can tie up emotions of fear, envy, and rage.

An early appearance of 'isolated' members is no disaster, but can provide an opportunity for group members to develop their attitudes on issues such as shyness, loneliness, and their own connection to or separation from others. When isolation is dealt with as a social dynamic, the stress then becomes not on the isolate, but on the reaction of the group to the isolate. Who in the group, for instance, is most concerned about the isolate? Isolates, instead of being a blight, can be reconstrued as a boon by the director, and a sociometry formed around the issue (state) or person (star). He or she can ask:

Stand next to the person whom you think is most concerned about Mick's isolation (star). OR

Put your hand on the shoulder of the person who you think could most help Mick's isolation (star). OR

Stand on a line between 1 and 100 according to your concern for Mick's isolation (state). OR

'Mary, who in the group is most concerned that Mick seems to be isolated? Who is next most concerned? Who isn't bothered by it at all?' (mixed state-star)

Secondly, isolation, like all other roles, does not necessarily represent the complete or permanent role constellation for any given person. The sociometric advantages of isolation in the current context need to be considered, as do the restraints (in the person and from the group) of taking on different roles. Questions can be asked around these issues:

Monty, if Mick were not so apart and apparently friendless, how do you think the group would be different?

Mal, what do you think the group would worry about if it were not worrying about Mick?

The rationale for this type of questioning, which may seem a little startling at this stage, will be developed in the chapter on 'Strategic sociometry'.

A non-strategic way of considering isolation is to regard it merely as a matter of inadequate warm-up to the task in hand. Let us imagine that the group warm-up involves a discussion concerning early relationships with teachers (of which the 'hidden theme', of course, might be the relationship of the group members to the leader). The leader notices that there are people who do not contribute to the discussion. They may be isolates, they may be uninterested, they may want to deal with other things, they may be desperately frightened, or they may be what used to be called 'shy', The director can address one of these people directly: 'I'd like to know about the sort of experiences you've had with teachers in your primary school'. If the person still sits and stares, it is almost certainly preferable not to force the issue. Instead, an invitation and a hidden command (see section on 'Strategic sociometry') can be offered. Or the director can say:

'Well, people are going to come up and do some things about teachers which will remind you and you may get some new ideas,'

Alternatively, the role of the isolate can be extended, and an injunction given to keep on doing what he or she is already doing, since that is what makes the most sense at the moment. The person's isolated system is given empathic definition from the 'outside', as it were:

'You may be sitting there, wondering what is going on; perhaps thinking you have made sense of it, perhaps thinking that it doesn't make sense at all. I personally think that it is possibly dangerous, and certainly illogical, to act against one's best interests. Many of the things I do, and many of the reactions of the other group members will surprise you, and you can hold your counsel even more tightly while you reflect on them.'

Sometimes one can do little other than leave isolated people alone, as they indicate their wishes to be so. Directors may need to watch their own anxiety about isolation, and to have reasonable confidence they are acting for the benefit of the isolate, rather than out of their own difficulties at apparent disapproval, or fear that they are 'failing' if not everyone participates in the group ethos. The interactional nature even of isolation itself always needs to be kept in mind. People can become isolated in a group for several reasons, including so-called scapegoating by other members, inappropriate activities on the part of the leader, or the positive intention of the leader in keeping him or herself apart.

The isolates' isolation, just as the gregarious person's sociability, is a result of their beliefs and feelings about what is going on: how they construe the situation. Their constructions of the situation may stem from roles that they have developed in their family-of-origin, or may stem from their current interactions. Everyone in the group is making sense of the situation as best they can, and no one needs to be taught to regard themselves as 'mad' or 'bad' by a persecution posing as therapy. Some people may even want, at particular times of their life, to consider themselves as mad or bad – so lonely that not even therapy, not even psychodrama, can 'help' them.

It is not useful to conduct an investigation of isolation as if that were simply a characteristic 'within' the person. Isolation, like nearly everything else, is social in its origins and in its effects. That is to say, a role is social in its origins and effects, a point which has been developed extensively in *The Passionate Technique* and here. For isolated, angry, or shy people to change their role, therefore (assuming they want to do so), the social factors in the group need to be addressed. This is where a group can exercise considerable leverage for good or ill. What is required is not that the individual changes, but that the group can do the work it set out to do. Group factors can be addressed directly, by means of sociometry or some form of 'encounter', or indirectly by means of psychodramas, or by other activities that alter the group theme and change the dynamics of interaction between individuals.

Chapter eleven

Sociometry as intervention

One should always start out on the wrong foot.

Carl Whitaker

When the lively light of spontaneity shines in a group, solutions that could previously not occur to members now become more obvious. By engaging with what *is* in the moment, they can at last act. Their imagination is expanded; they can see pathways that were not available to them before, feel whatever is to be felt, and *move*. Ideally, they begin to operate in the present, using their existing responses more flexibly or summoning new ones.

Their old story has been deeply etched with forbidden agendas (usually imposed by relationships) on believing something different from their 'lived experience'. Relationships always involve feeling and action as well; so new information implies new relationships. Any reforming of relationships will happen most readily when participants come alive to all of their current experience in those relationships – their beliefs, their feelings, their actions. Changes in relationship mean not simply changes in world-views, but development in the actions of each person and connectedness to important events in society. This chapter focuses on sociometry as an intervention that not only measures but affects the world-views and relationships of members of a group.

We live in symbol and language; that is what 'meaning' is. It is obvious, therefore, that the language of a criterion question itself will produce significant effects in a group. Even in everyday life, if one person says to another, 'How is your mother?' they are producing at least some warm-up in the other person to their family-of-origin. Whether or not the other person wishes to reply, or resents the question, or does not know how their mother is anyway, they must go through a series of images until they come to the one, 'mother'. You can see that requests for information can also be transmissions of information, or commands to access a certain state. The old sure-fire wager 'I bet you cannot not think about elephants for the next thirty seconds' illustrates a similar process.

When asking a question or conducting an exercise, therefore, the information that a group leader seeks to 'draw from' the group simultaneously 'puts in' data. You may recall that in the Introduction I suggested that the archaeological 'dig' of a drama was as much 'plant' as 'dig'. Indeed, co-creation in a group has been a theme of this book. So it will come as no surprise to you to consider that an exercise on intimacy, for example, actually begins a self-questioning process for each member around a particular topic (in this case intimacy) whether or not that is what people were originally concerned with. That is the whole intention, though of course the exercise may be well- or ill-timed, appropriate or not. Take another example: a director who asks: 'Who in the group is most capable of looking after themselves . . . stand on a line from 0 to 100' is apparently requesting information, but is also introducing the concept 'Looking after yourself'.

The director may want actively to warm up the whole group to that issue, or to find a protagonist, or to test an hypothesis about a central concern of the group. Members begin to conceptualize themselves in terms of 'being able to look after' themselves. Their conceptualization will be different if the criterion is 'most prone to look after other people', and different again if the criterion is 'unwilling to look after other people'. Not only is a measure being exacted, but a concept is introduced. If that concept is introduced often enough, it can become a group norm, for example, of 'taking care of others'. Here are some other examples of sociometric exercises and questions that embed commands in the transmission of information:

With the traumatic events of the last week, how did you manage to support each other? Those who supported each other mostly because of basic loyalties go to this end; those who supported each other because of trusting each others' inner strength go to this end.

In two years' time, when this problem is sorted out, and is ancient history, who will be the person to have learnt the most?

Stand on a line from here . . . to here according to how much you're using your energy not to be fully present at the moment.

It is obvious, then, that sociometric criterion questions influence what they observe. They produce certain states in the group – effectively becoming embedded commands: 'Be this'. An embedded command is a suggestion whose qualities are hidden in language. For example, the instruction: 'Go over to the group member who is most like your best friend when you are in Grade 5' will not only produce the required activity, but will also tend to have the effect of making the members 'return' to that period in their lives. In other words, the question produces a temporary state of age regression in the group; it implies 'Be ten years old'. The group begins to operate patterns which are not ordinarily conscious, though the response, in the action of going across to someone who is similar to an early playmate, is apparently a completely 'conscious' and ordinary one.

Constructing hypotheses

Sociometric procedures not only indicate factors such as 'isolation', which was the focus of the preceding chapter. They may also point to the existence of persons in the group who are available to assist with integration of the group into a more cohesive unit. One way to identify a 'cleavage' between sub-groups, suggests Hale (1974), is to ask all group members to form two or more informal groups to accomplish a simple task; for example, to discuss a certain issue. From the emergent sub-groupings, the director can then ask members to account for the groupings which they made. The answers that members give, such as 'these are the people I trust', or 'these are the most fun to be with', or whatever, can provide material for systemic hypotheses on the state of the group. The questions around these hypotheses need not only follow one theme, but can cover several issues, though the themes of the members of the sub-groupings will tend to converge, no matter what the topic.

Criteria need to be based on hypotheses about what is occurring in the group at any stage. In fact, hypothesis-based criteria are the most worthwhile of all: others are allowable as shots-in-the-dark when necessary, or as warm-ups, but the ones that 'tell' are those based on a shrewd guess at the group's central concern. Here are some questions you can ask yourself when you are constructing an hypothesis:

1. *What is the movement between this session and previous sessions?*
2. *What is the group central concern at the moment?*
3. *Who are the stars and who are the rejectees? Why?*
4. *Towards whom do I feel personally drawn? Why is this?*
5. *Whose eye am I avoiding? Why?*
6. *What are my own fantasies and warm-ups right now?*
7. *What are the alliances and coalitions, and what are possible reasons for them?*
8. *When did this particular theme start? Who is promoting it; who is avoiding it?*

9. Who is protecting whom, or making themselves 'less' so that someone else can be 'more'? How does this fit with what I know already?

Through these and other types of questions, directors seek a genuinely systemic understanding of the group. The hypotheses are held lightly, and are designed to lead to constructive action, rather than to 'pathologizing' or labelling.

Let us say that an overt group theme is 'anger' (people are disagreeing with each other a lot, or else they are narrating incidents, apparently disconnected, in which someone damaged them), while the underlying theme appears to be 'fear'. Sociometric criteria based first on anger and then on fear can then be devised. When directors, therefore, wish to bring information to the group about sensitivity to or the management of anger, they can ask 'Who in the group. . .?' questions such as 'Who in the group is most in touch with/most warmed up to/most capable of expressing, their anger?' or 'Towards whom in the group do you feel most free to express angry feelings?' The same sorts of questions can then be asked about fear, providing an anger/fear link, if that is how the director sees it. Negative explanation can be provided in the form of questions on the restraints on change: 'What or who stops you/other from experiencing your/their anger or fear?'

The procedure, then, is that directors first make their own analysis of the links between various topics, themes, and apparent alliances. They present the hypothesized link to the group in the form of a series of criterion questions. The group then confirms or disconfirms the hypothesis, and is able to warm up more directly to the themes than when they were obscure. Whatever the result, they arrive at their understandings through their own choices, and their own observations of the alliances and sub-groupings. They can then discuss what they have done in pairs in the whole group. A soundly-based protagonist-centred or a group-centred psychodrama might result from this strong systemic matrix.

The questions can also take a 'spectogram' format, such as 'Stand on a line up this end if you feel free to express your anger/fear, and down this end if you do not feel so free'. A spectogram does not reveal stars, but it does show where people locate themselves on a given issue. Alliances of agreement or disagreement also become evident by this process, and the spectogram can lead directly into action; it is an action in itself, of course.

The point of conducting a formal sociometry is that a director not only can test many hypotheses about the group by physical methods, but also he or she can use sociometric procedures as an educative device, actually teaching various norms and links between role states in an active yet unobtrusive way. The 'lesson' is truly heartfelt, when emotion, thinking, and action come together. In sociometry one actually does lay oneself 'on the line'.

Family-of-origin sociometric activities

The aim of sociometry is to reveal and then to clean up systems so that they become productive, and open to information-exchange from the outside. At the beginning of a group, it may be necessary to look inwards at the circle so that the social atom has a chance to form. But sooner or later members need to turn outwards for information. If the group is a therapy group, of course, its aim is to do away with itself altogether.

Sociometric exercises need not only be about the here-and-now of the group, nor need they be run directly by the leader once he or she has set them up. Displaced roles from the original social atom can serve as warm-ups to the present, and these can be revealed by sociometric exercises such as the following:

In a psychodrama that you might enact about your life at the moment, what would be the most important auxiliary role, and who in the group would you choose to fill it?

This kind of activity done in pairs, threes, or fours can be extremely useful and moving. It is close to 'social atom' work, in itself a form of sociometry. The exercise can have two effects: firstly, the actual sociometric results become evident, which can lead to further action about the type of personal constructs that are operating, and secondly, they act as embedded commands to warm up to family-of-origin. A drama can take off from either of these points, but this type of warm-up needs to have a soundly considered focus. After all, anyone can get upset about their family-of-origin, and a warm-up to pain, while easy to effect, can ultimately be exploitative. An exercise that does not steer a person so tightly in one direction is the following:

Take your notebooks, find a partner and sit down with him or her. Talk to each other for a short time about your family when you were about seven – who was there, where you lived, etc. Now consider a time when you're very frightened . . . who would you be most likely to have been soothed by when you were that age? Draw a diagram of people at various distances from you according to who could soothe you.

This exercise is a very complex one in terms of its intended effects. Although it overtly concerns the past, it is actually implanting a norm within the group and within people's life in their outside social atom. It does not reinforce notions of being a victim in one's family; rather, it stresses the practical things one can do when another is frightened or anxious.

The advantages of this method are several: everyone in the group has time to develop a sociometry of a particular stage of their life; people become therapists to each other; a therapeutic concept is unobtrusively introduced, that of 'being soothed when one is anxious'; and the sociometry is written down, or diagrammatic, leading to a different, perhaps 'right brain' way of understanding one's early childhood. Different levels of consciousness are involved when one talks or draws or acts, and so the meaning of 'reality' derived from these three modes is altered somewhat by the mode itself. In the case of the drawings of social atom, any resulting strong warm-ups that are unable to be managed in the dyads can later be dealt with by the director, possibly in the form of a psychodrama.

Still keeping the notion (and embedded command) of 'being soothed', another exercise could be developed with similar instructions for pairs to assist each other, retaining the age of seven as a relevant period:

Starting with your father, draw a role diagram of when you were seven for each member of your family showing by whom they were soothed when they were anxious. Tell your partner how this soothing was done.

With this exercise, one moves more into the area of strategic sociometry. Although no structural analysis is actually made, some of the structure of the protagonist's family of origin is likely to become clear. To draw the diagram from the point of view of each family member involves, of course, a mental role reversal. The family system becomes revealed from many angles: the amount of 'soothing' that goes on in the family at large and the differences between members on this issue are also revealed. The exercise has therefore achieved many aims: to introduce the notion of 'soothing' in a family by means of an embedded command; to have people working together as co-therapists; to reveal a family sociometry around the criterion; to produce a degree of regression; to reveal differences between various family cultures, and to reveal differences between family-of-origin belief systems and the current beliefs of one member. The member may begin to assess how much they value 'soothing' versus how much 'soothing when distressed' was part of the family culture.

Directors who have a thorough understanding of sociometry, and think in terms of systems, can tailor a paired sociogram on the spot. For example, the director might judge that the group is undergoing a state of anxiety about independence, and is reproducing a very early stage of mirroring their mothers' anxiety. There are many psychodramatic ways in which this topic can be approached, but a start can be made sociometrically. Having a focus on the protagonist of the diagram, the following exercise could be given:

When you were very little, and you wanted to explore, who in the family was most confident that you could do that? Draw all of them in terms of being most confident about your exploration. OR

Set out a row of chairs to represent your relatives' confidence about your ability to explore. Address each of them in turn.

Here the focus changes from 'soothing when one is anxious' to an emphasis on confidence about being an individual. The stress this time is on exploration and support rather than on anxiety. While the members are drawing in their dyads, they are actually manufacturing information about appropriate parental attachment. Each individual in the pair is likely to have had different experiences of being parented, and so can learn from the other by comparing their different social atoms. The very fact of the members working in pairs at this stage also helps to dump the notion that the only way to get one's needs met is through parents, or through their surrogate: the director. Hence the individuation content of the exercise is reinforced through its form.

The great themes of psychology can be introduced by means of sociometry because as much information is being supplied as being elicited. The information is often that which the members already have, though they do not know it. But it is organized around concepts that may be news to the members in the ways they think about themselves – being soothed, curiosity, attachment, freedom, and so on. There are few limits to what can be asked: one could make Eric Erikson's life stages cycle into sociometries, by asking various questions of members about various stages of their lives, and couching the criteria in Eriksonian terms:

When you were seven, who in the family. . . .
When you were sixteen, who in the family. . . .
When you were twenty-two. . . .

The director may observe quite intense warm-ups in the group during this type of exercise – indeed any family-of-origin exercise. The process can easily lead to a psychodrama around such themes as bonding, restriction, curiosity, or independence. Such a psychodrama will tend to have a strong impact on the group members, who have been thoroughly warmed-up to the theme by the exercises they have already done in pairs, and they will tend to share richly afterwards. The group dynamic may also alter, as if a developmental stage has been 'worked through' by everybody. Neither psychodrama nor any other therapy can within one session deal conclusively with such an important issue as 'attachment', but the sociometric method opens the way in terms of the system's re-adjustment and spontaneity required. All groups and all therapies constantly return to this issue, in its many forms.

Chapter twelve

Sociometric applications

It is the business of the future to be dangerous.

A. N. Whitehead

Sociometry to start a group

Both here and in *The Passionate Technique* I have worked within a Batesonian framework: well-couched requests for information lead to news of difference, which help weaken the restraints, or forbidden agendas, binding people to think only in certain ways. If this is so, then sociometric procedures are far from the simple measuring devices that they appear to be. They also produce information about differences; they teach, engender attitudes, act as commands, and serve to warm up the group in a particular direction. Although they may demonstrate what the warm-up is, they are, in effect, interventions with the potential to alter warm-up and produce new kinds of thinking (spontaneity). Now that some of the norm-setting factors embedded in the language of sociometric directive are a little clearer, let us go right back to when a group first meets, and devise some life-giving first-time sociometric exercises.

Not only does each individual have a set of roles within a group, but the group itself seems to develop a set of roles, or group constructs. A group forms its own belief system, mythology, and symptomatology. As a whole, it can have the role of 'Rebellious Child' for example, or 'Soggy Mass' or 'Ingratiating Salesman'. Reader, the 'pattern that connects' connects so quickly. It can happen as people walk through the door; sometimes it seems to happen before they walk in the door. Because the group so rapidly becomes a 'little society', sociometric procedures can be applied from the outset, even though actual acquaintance among members is very slight. Right from the start, people are reacting to each other, basing their responses on non-verbal signals, projections, intuition, and speech. The power of these fantasized and sometimes misleading attributions can be quite durable, long after contradictory information could have changed them. Perhaps because the 'business of the future' is so dangerous, they have become part of the group myth, and can be relatively unshakeable.

If it is true that we only know things by similarity and difference, then it makes sense that sociometry at the beginning of a group should be designed to identify commonalities – similar backgrounds, opinions, existing friendships with the other members, or level of experience in groups. These sociometric procedures are not simply clever ways of getting people into pairs, but are in themselves an exploration of the demography of the group according to specific criteria. Each member gets a sense of where he or she fits in; at the same time, each member fits in a little more as a result of the new definitions and distinctions.

Beginning sociometries can be so informal that people do not know they are happening. Even reading off a list of who is attending the group, and asking that person to stand up is an ultra-unobtrusive sociometric. It serves the purpose of actually allowing the group leader to see who is present, but its main aim might be to greet that person and make them visible to the rest of the group. At the absolute beginning of the group, it can be the first step to knitting the group together. It forms a link between the members and director, especially as greetings are exchanged or some question is asked ('Where are you from?') after each name is called.

Another extremely 'ordinary' and informal procedure is to ask 'Who here is from the country?' When those people indicate, they can be asked when or if they left, and so forth. Similar questions can be asked about members' town of origin: 'Were you born there?. . . . There's no hospital. Oh, I see. So you were born in the city of . . . . Who else was born in that city?' and so on. These questions are not such as to frighten people, or overwhelm them with an unfamiliar 'psychology'. But the group unwittingly is gaining a sense of where people stand with each other, and are taking their first steps as actors. The process can be full of humour, surprises, and shifts of gear, yet one that subtly begins to lock the group together and warm it to its task. If the group in question is highly task-oriented, for whom these questions might seem disappointing frivolities, appropriate questions can be generated concerning origins and identity, such as 'Who has been with this company more than ten years . . . between five and ten?', and so on. Australian director Max Clayton is expert at this unobtrusive sociometry.

Whatever the nature of the group, sociometric procedures can be conducted concerning the members' group histories.

Stand here if this is your first group. . . . Now stand here those of you who have done between two and five of these groups before. . . . Stand here those of you who have had experience in more than five groups of this nature.

Each person can then be briefly interviewed (while they are standing in their positions – the interview by that very fact becomes drama) about their experiences in various groups. Or better, 'old timers' can be asked to share their wisdom with the 'greenhorns'. This procedure makes overt the hierarchical concerns with which people tend to be preoccupied at the beginning of groups – their respective level of experience and whether or not they are likely to be bored or overwhelmed, whether or not they will be integrated into the group.

Other active ways of achieving a similar result might take the following form:

Form a line from here to here (indicates). Position yourself up this end if you know more than ten people in this group. Stand down this end if you know one or none. Put yourself along the line according to how many people you know.

The line can then be used to form pairs or larger groups. Instructions can be given for members to talk to the person next to them on the line, or for people from one end of the line to talk to people at the other end. These or similar exercises are appropriate at this stage because, at the beginning of a group, identity and inclusion issues are paramount. Not much can happen in terms of the work of the group until people have had some chance to settle their concerns about inclusion, where they stand vis-à-vis others. Such concerns are perennial, of course, but they are particularly prominent when a group is beginning.

It is customary, once a whole-group sociometry has been derived, for some sort of 'pairs' work to be suggested, so that all members have a chance to express themselves about the information that has been revealed, and so that their sense of self can be reaffirmed. These aims will be best achieved by their forming a 'real' relationship with someone – contact that has a depth which would be impossible to achieve with the whole group at this stage. Even though the 'pairs' work may be quite fleeting, people do feel they are on solid ground when they speak with one other person, if only to express surprise that so many/few people know more than ten people in the group, or apprehension/excitement about being a newcomer.

When each person has spoken, the director usually asks them to 'report in'. As has been suggested above, an early sociometric exercise for a newly formed group might well concern the number of people known to each other in the group – the 'acquaintance pattern'. The large group exercise is followed by a conversation with the next person along the line, and that may be followed by meeting and greeting selected others from up and down the line. The person most connected in terms of old friendships might greet the person who is the most complete stranger to everyone. Or people who had indicated that they knew very few others may be encouraged to greet each other, and so forth.

The actual specifics of the formula – who greets whom – are not so important as the process of greeting and assurance and suppleness in the members as they begin to feel no longer 'alone'. The greeting is itself an 'action' as is the act of standing on the line in the first place. Suddenly all members are not only actors, but they have speaking parts too. This achievement may sound a trivial one, but it is a big step for some people, and it makes a great difference – as anyone who has suffered a group that is shy, stuck, and moribund will testify. Whatever their form, these procedures are usually preferable to asking what people 'do', and where they come from; such questions tend to reproduce conventional hierarchies and further develop rigid habits of interaction which will be unhelpful if the group is designed to induce spontaneity.

A second linear sociometry may be produced after the first, the criterion of which would usually concern the goals of the workshop or new group. If the goals of the group are left too long in abeyance, people tend to become suspicious of the motives of the leader, and begin to feel 'psychologized'. They have come to this workshop or group for a purpose, and it ill behoves a leader to play hide-and-seek with them. Leaders who are ambiguous or mysterious about the goals of the group will certainly be able to induce rapid regression as a result of members being confused at the apparent failure of an authority. But aside from aggrandizing their own power by increasing regressive dependence, it is quite uncertain what benefit such veiled intentions bring to the group.

A standard second sociometric criterion, therefore, might be based on people's background and experiences relative to the purpose of the group. Members may already have covertly compared themselves with others on these criteria anyway, as 'knowing the ropes' is an implicit criterion for sociometric stardom early on in a group, just as it is for any beginning venture – we might remember this from school playground days onward. 'Knowing the ropes' early on is believed (usually wrongly) to determine issues of inclusion and exclusion. The linear sociometry that is enacted answers the question, 'Where do I fit in?' An example has already been given of a 'prior experience' criterion, and how to follow it up. Here is another, suitable for a professional or training group in psychology:

Stand HERE if your essential experience is in groupwork; HERE if your chief experience is in drama; HERE if your background is in psychodrama, and HERE if your work is mostly clinically based with individuals.

Naturally, some people will want to be in two or more of these groups, and can thereby provide links between them. A person in one group can then be asked to call out to a person in another about why they are in the workshop from the point of view of their background. The director encourages a person from a third group to respond to these two, and so on. A sharp eye needs to be kept so that the discussion does not become bogged down, and so that the original impetus and excitement of moving about is kept up. Any linear sociometry can easily lead into a form of action, and can be deepened in terms of personal warm-up:

In pairs, find an object in the room that represents a comment on your position. Locate yourself in respect to that object and interact with it with the help of your partner. OR

Make a drawing of how people from your original social atom would react to seeing you at that point on that line. Say something to those people.

If the group members are too unskilled to do these exercises in pairs, the object can still be chosen or the drawing still be done, but the director can manage the interaction. Sometimes this activity in itself can lead to a group mini-sociodrama, which can be a very satisfying and appropriate result. Or, if the group is a training workshop for the helping professions, the director can say:

Form a line. Stand here if you are here for personal reasons, and here if you are here for professional reasons.

When that has been done the director might say, 'What does one mean by "professional"? What if "professional" meant the intellectual and emotional understanding of social systems. See if you want to change your position on the line.' This twin sociometry in rapid succession can have the effect of usefully breaking up people's rigid constructs. The result may not be so powerful if the definition of 'professional' had been offered first off. The twin format actually causes people to retrace with their feet their new thinking.

The third sociometric exercise, if the director wishes to go that far, may well be concerned with warm-up itself. How urgent is a particular personal or professional issue for each member? Who are the people ready to be actors at this early stage? To avoid the line (now paling in its novelty) a series of circles may be introduced, perhaps with a cushion in the centre. The instruction can be given:

In the centre of the room there is a cushion, representing absolute urgency to work on this (planning/personal growth purpose of the workshop) issue. Stand in circles around the cushion depending on how hot you are to get going. Nearest is very hot; outer circles are cooler.

Thus, a tripartite standard sociometry 'package' for a beginning group might involve acquaintance with others, background/experience, and readiness for work.

Illustration no. 1: professional identity

Dot has been charged with the task of running the first formal session of a conference. The conference is made up of people from several professional organizations who are involved in student services. There are OTs, social workers, speech therapists, psychologists, medicos, and nurses. After a few preliminary 'Stand on a line' sociometries to reveal basic likenesses, familiarity with the method, how hungover they are, etc. (it is Day 1 of the conference, following registration and drinks the night before), Dot takes by the hand a professional from one area, let us say an OT, and leads her to one part of the room. She then takes a medico, and leads her to another part. She does the same with the other professions, in a mysterious manner. Then she says to the rest of the group: ' Join the person who represents your area of work.'

Each discrete group then selects one of their members to be the representative of the profession ('a typical OT', 'a typical psychologist', etc.). These 5 or 6 meet anxiously, while their former team-mates conjure up a typical incident involving the typical client in a typical case for that profession. Then, in front of the whole group, the typical OT meets the typical OT client for a brief encounter amidst much laughter and egging on. When these meetings are done, the whole group joins together to discuss the typical interactions that have been shown.

Dot found this simple procedure extremely effective to give 'presence' to the different professional areas and the work they did. She commented that as well as building up the professional profile of each person, simultaneously the barriers of suspicion and sheer lack of knowledge were broken down between people. The apparent gratuitousness of the exercise served not so much as an icebreaker, but as a solid and efficient lead-in to a complex topic.

Illustration no. 2: client–helper systems

Dot's preliminary sociometry schema was developed into a whole day's consultancy by Duane and Duke, who frequently worked together with educational groups. In this instance, the referring body was a diverse set of professionals from many organizations whose work area concerned disadvantaged youth. Present were social workers, lawyers, youth workers, psychologists, employment officers, and so on.

Duane and Duke conducted preliminary sociometries in a way somewhat similar to Dot's work. Each professional group was gathered in a different area of the room, and encouraged to warm up to a 'typical' client, and briefly to conduct an enactment. But the work was deepened and extended by more formal interview-in-role of each client, which developed an idea of why they were attending the professional, what their beliefs were about being helped, and so on. Other more psychodramatic techniques were then employed such as maximization, which produced vivid and fruitful interactions between the typical client and the typical worker.

Not only was each profession able to see what the others did, as in Dot's group, but the professional groups had the chance to experience role reversal with their clients, and gain entry to the ways in which they construed the world. In some cases, the procedures led to a cathartic solution. In other cases, the social system of the client and the help-giver was included for more dispassionate role analysis, so that those present began to appreciate more the client–helper system, rather than merely the client system or merely the helper system.

Duane and Duke's use of preliminary sociometry suggests that sociometric procedures are probably underused in consulting and even psychodramatic work. In these examples, the professional sociometry of the present group is briefly evoked ('Gather in your occupational areas') and then the sociometry of a further group – the clients – is joined on. Even simple sociometries can get at the logic of organizations and the institutional, as well as the emotional, reasons for people's actions. The intimate anarchy of the exercises enlivens what would otherwise be banal data-gathering, and immediately suggests directions for further work.

Notional sociometries

A sociometric choice does not need always to be acted out physically. The mind can do its own travelling. For instance, let us suppose the group is divided into pairs: each partner can be asked by the director to imagine him or herself on a position on an imaginary line representing a particular criterion, and then to tell (or not tell – the actual communication is customary but not a necessary part of sociometric choice) their partner where they would stand on that line. Likewise (and more in terms of strategic sociometry) they can be asked to 'guess' where their partner would be standing on the line. In fact, there is no need to limit oneself to lines – this is just one form of sociometry. An instruction could be given:

If you were feeling a bit serious and wanted to have a really good laugh, who in the group would help you to laugh? Tell your partner. OR

If you were finding it hard to talk in this group, who here might be best able to help you express yourself? Don't just judge by people you know; use your intuition.

In each of these cases, the sociometry is so far 'notional': it is not acted out in front of the whole group. These private procedures in pairs may be slightly less frightening for a group that is new to this sort of thing than it would be actually going over and standing next to the selected person, although this latter action is always an option if the director thinks some good purpose would be served.

When directors decide on a sociometric criterion, ideally the basis of the criterion is a certain hypothesis about the state of the group. Randomly chosen criteria can warm the group up to many issues; if the warm-up is too diffuse, the group will lose spontaneity and tend to become bewildered, flat, and dependent. If the director then berates members for their dependence, they may become even more so, although the original 'cause' of it may have been the poor structures set up by the leader in the first place.

Sociometry in an established group

Sociometric exercises are not difficult to design: all one needs is a grasp of sociometric principles and a deeply-held belief that it is culture which exercises power over the psyche, rather than the other way round. The most commonly used sociometric exercises when the group has been under way for some time generally concern the here-and-now processes of the group. They might entail themes of *identification*, the general form of which is 'Who in the group is most like you in some way?' This general form can become specific if the director actually identifies the criterion of likeness:

Who in the group most represents a role that you would like to to develop?

Who in the group prominently has roles that you think are overdeveloped in yourself?

Questions about *alliances* in the group reveal its basic ideological and companionship structures. The goal of sociometric enquiry into alliances is not simply to reveal the alliances, but also to provide information that makes a difference. So the net effect of the enquiry is first to reveal, and then, by the simple fact of the new information being available, to allow new alliances to form.

From whom in the group could you most easily accept feedback. . .? Whose feedback would it be the hardest to accept?

Go and stand next to the person you would be most likely to telephone afterwards if you had a bad session in the group.

Put your hand on the shoulder of the person with whom you feel most safe.

Put your hand on the shoulder of the person in the group with whom you feel most conflict at the moment.

Stand next to the person with whom you feel you have the most intimate relationship.

Minibus

People seem to learn rapidly when they are active, and when their behaviour, which has seemed random, after all turns out to have been consistent. The idea for the group drama reported below arose by chance in a group meeting one day. At the beginning of the session, several members had been, as usual, late. Those present were discussing, in a desultory fashion, how people actually travelled to the group: some people drove alone, others car-shared with one other person, and two groups came four-to-a-car. The question arose as to whether this detracted from group 'energy', allowing sub-groups and 'pairing' to take place. Sub-groups are regarded as dangerous in the group literature, as they are said to enable people to manage their anxiety and therefore cool down their warm-up.

The chief topic, however, became the issue of inclusion/exclusion, and specifically whether the people who arrived and left in fours formed a sort of 'special club' whose members were always loyal to each other. The punctual people were worried that the others spent long and luxurious debriefing hours after a session on the way home, and were able to get their version of reality 'right' before a session began, thus forming a 'block' opinion on events and 'excluding the little guy'.

One of the members, May, a woman who, as it happened, came to the group alone, had a minibus. Another member, Mollie, said jokingly, 'Why don't we all come in May's minibus, and then there wouldn't be all this fuss about sub-groups?' The director asked Mollie to set up May's minibus and then to locate the group members on the various benches in it 'as she saw it'.

This Mollie did, establishing one person as the driver, and arranging other people on the front, middle, and rear seats. Four members of the group she left out of the bus, saying that she could not visualize them being in there at all.

The session could have progressed in this form for some time – a kind of visual analogue for Mollie's group social atom. However, this procedure of one person setting out all the other people in the group from their point of view usually starts off in an interesting way, and then flattens out, in the author's experience.

The unwitting sociometric implications of Mollie's scene were becoming evident to the director, who changed the instruction, addressing all the group members: 'Don't worry about where Mollie has put you – simply take up a position on the bus that suits you best. Sit with whoever you want to sit, and in whatever position.' Mollie herself, and the four members who had been left out of the bus, were also invited to join it.

Gradually people got used to the new instruction, and to the notion that they could sit where they liked. They could sit where they like in the group, of course, but here the choice appeared larger and more significant, probably because the format was now that of drama.

After a while, some people began to change their positions on the bus, and some remained where they were. The driver, for example, kept driving. The man in the back seat stayed there. A woman who got on in the front seat, which seemed to represent a type of responsible or even 'parental' position, also stayed there, but kept looking around wistfully at the people in the middle. This middle group comprised a very active, writhing mass who appeared to be having a wonderful time; only one woman had got out of it, and when the positions were 'liberated', went to the back seat, where she sat quietly. But others had come from various places on the bus to the centre bench. They were rolling over each other, throwing orange peels, and laughing.

When the group had settled in relatively stable positions, the director then 'froze' the action and began interviewing. Each person was asked why they had originally chosen the position they were in, and why then remained in that position, if they stayed, or why they have moved, if they moved. They were also asked what it felt like to be where they were.

When the person replied, the director helped them interpret what they said in terms of their roles in the group. He then asked the other members of the bus (who are all still seated in their positions) how what the speaker said fitted into their perceptions of him or her. These observations were also translated into role terms. The way was then clear for an on-the-spot role analysis based on overdeveloped, underdeveloped, conflicted, or adequate roles.

The person had already demonstrated in action and by choice at least part of their sociometric position in the group. Other people reacted to this choice, confirming or disconfirming the choice in terms of their perceptions of that person and their roles in the group. The informal role analysis can then be made more formal by the director, who may ask the members to attempt role titles for the person's major roles. Finally, gaps in the role analysis can themselves suggest developmental possibilities. The person is thus saved from developing roles that are already highly developed (for example, Intimate Sharer) and that may have become problem-causing attempted solutions (that is, when in difficulties, the person's solution may be to 'share' even more intimately, even though this is the last thing that the situation calls for).

Minibus was far from a simple form of sociometry, containing as it did quite strong elements of a group drama. As has been remarked before, such exercises best follow from a hypothesis about the state of the group, or else lead to such an hypothesis. In the case of Minibus, the group was, in fact, debilitated by a series of alliances which seemed largely based on sub-groups using the same car. These sub-groups exercised considerable power in the group by always arriving late: the forbidden agenda involved alliances which, although originally and innocently based on convenience, did provide a form of 'flight'. A drama held later that day confirmed that notion. Minibus acted as a changer of the group sociometry – shaking it out of its rigid form, and bringing more freshness and sanity to the regrouping.

Chapter thirteen

Strategic sociometry

Those who wish to be right and prove you wrong have never interested me in the long run. I prefer juggling to throwing and catching.

Kate Llewellyn

When a dramatic event occurs in a group, each person, naturally enough, forms an opinion on what happened. Narrative and opinion become inseparable; they are 'stories', and can be given the status of sacred truth. Forms of 'group story' are then created in the group in order to explain what is happening in the now; present and past interact in a way that shapes the narrative even further. Consider the following example of an interaction in a training group.

Mollie has just had a heated confrontation with Maria. The group, in fact, has been having a lot of rows over recent weeks, and this is one of many such outbreaks, some of which Duane has developed psychodramatically. Although the actual fight is over, it is in danger of being pasted into the group mythology by the Mollie faction as 'Whenever anyone speaks out here, they're not supported' and by the Maria faction as 'You can't even breathe here without getting attacked'. The work of the group does not appear to be getting done.

Duane has several options: to direct the encounter psychodramatically, by expanding Mollie's and Maria's roles to the fullest; to make group-as-a-whole interpretations on the state of the group; to make personal interpretations to Mollie or Maria about the dynamics of their behaviour; to spread the encounter between the participants among other group members; or to ignore the whole incident and see what happens next.

Duane does not do any of these things. He believes that the fight is not so much an expression of spontaneity as a manifestation of the group becoming stuck in a 'fight' mode. That is, he conjectures that the point of the incident may lie outside the expressed hostility between Mollie and Maria. He decides to test this hypothesis by directing the group's attention away from the two people involved. He asks Bob:

Bob, when Mollie gets angry, does Cindy feel closer to Lucy or further away?
Lucy, does Bob feel more relieved before the outburst, or after it?

The quotation from Kate Llewellyn at the start of this chapter seems to fit: this type of procedure is certainly more like juggling than throwing and catching. Nor is there any attempt to prove one person right and the other wrong. By asking these questions of people in the group other than Mollie or Maria, Duane is acting on a circular rather than a linear model of cause-and-effect. That is why he does not at first address the principal characters of the incident directly; rather, he asks 'around', special types of questions involving comparisons (Cecchin, 1987; Selvini Palazzoli *et al.*, 1980; Penn, 1982; Sanders, 1985; Tomm, 1984).

Duane's questions themselves convey to the group a systemic understanding: not 'X does this'; but 'What Y does when X does this'. He believes in 'co-evolution': no part of the system, for example Judith, has only one-way influence over any other part of the system. The behaviour of any 'part', such as Mollie herself, or the Mollie/Maria dyad, is highly influenced by the behaviour of the other parts. It is also influenced, of course, by its own previous behaviour, the stories it has already told itself about what is happening. Since the influence is circular, Duane believes that his inquiry must also be circular.

This chapter attempts to link what Duane does as a co-evolutionist with more standard sociometric practices that you may be more used to. As this is a central chapter on strategic groupwork, it contains a summary of many of the ideas presented already. It does so in a framework of 'co-evolution', 'difference', and 'shifting the frame of thought'. You may find your head spinning a little, and yourself going into a bit of a daze. Do not worry too much: it is the material itself, most likely. The circularity of reality, when described, tends to be entrancing.

Moreno remarks that sociometry is to a large extent a classificatory science which inquires 'into the evolution and organization of groups and the position of individuals within them.' (1953, p. 51). It is a *socius* (companion) *metrum* (measure). Duane's questioning is based on verbal estimates of similarities and differences, and therefore is in essence sociometric. Because his questions are usually asked to a third person, Duane's technique is a projective companion-measure.

Duane wishes the group to find out its alliances around a particular problem or incident. His method is similar to one that the Milan Associates (Selvini Palazzoli *et al.*, 1980) have called 'circular questioning', which they developed as a counter-move for families that were stuck. Their interviewing style aimed to provide the family with new ideas, especially concerning changes of relationships after a significant event. I am saying that similar ways of working can apply to groups that are stuck. When the Morenian and the Milanese methods are grafted and applied to a group setting, the result is 'strategic sociometry'.

Theoretical orientation

Fights in groups are sometimes a way of avoiding or delaying the 'work' that the group has been set up to do. A group goes through several developmental phases, each of which produces dilemmas for the members and the leader. Solutions to these dilemmas may be effective or ineffective, enabling or restrictive as you have already seen. When a group applies restrictive solutions to its dilemmas, it becomes 'stuck'. These solutions may take the form of 'dependency', 'fighting', 'fleeing', and 'pairing' (Bion, 1961). A group comes together to change, but develops 'basic assumptions' quite contrary to that purpose – indeed, its solutions may well help counteract the anxiety associated with changes to a new sort of story.

Now clearly some solutions are more restrictive than others; in fact, all solutions are in some way restrictive, and represent a compromise. One applies a solution as the best possible fit into what one sees as 'the reality of the situation'. Some labels on solutions, however, lose this sense of the person doing their best. The labels themselves become restrictive and punitive: 'anxiety', 'manic depressive', 'defences', 'avoiding intimacy' are some of them.

Individuals tend to act in ways that they regard as self-enhancing, and a group will do the same. Consider the solution of 'fighting', which was the one adopted by Mollie and Maria: when two people in a group fight, they enter into a kind of paradoxical alliance whereby they attempt to do what seems best at the time – to ward off overpowering personal attention ('avoid intimacy'), to get over frustrations, or to win the leader's attention and favour. They could even be trying to help out another member of the group who is depressed.

Duane tries to establish the function of the alliances in terms of what the reaction to them is in the larger group. He asks himself: 'If fighting is a solution, what is the problem? Does fighting maintain the problem rather than resolve it?' He may then ask the group a series of questions around this notion. These questions elicit information about what pairs are operating in the group, and furthermore, what the effect of those pairings is on the other group members. The questions could also produce information, as we have seen: for example, about feared disasters, the dangers that are evoked when one asks about the negative consequences of change, or the problems that would arise if the fighting stopped. This form of thinking may take some time to get used to.

Let us say that Duane finds that the members believe that a crisis in the group will stimulate cohesion. His questions would then track who believes that and who does not, who most/least fears that the group is disintegrating, who has most to gain from the fighting, and so on. Or suppose another function of the fight emerges: there is a consensus that the 'problem' in the group's development has been people's 'inability to deal with anger' (that is, they see it as preferable to absorb insults and criticism rather than more actively reacting to them), and that there are certain people to whom particularly the group responds in this respect. Questions around the issue of anger can be asked to any member:

Carol, who notices first when someone is beginning to get angry? Jim, who is most relieved in this group when someone blows their stack?

Following these questions, Duane can move the whole group into action, either by asking members to 'place yourself on a line as to how relieved you are when someone blows their stack' (a 'spectogram') or he can ask selected people to respond directly to Mollie, or to Jim's choice of 'who was most relieved' ('perceptual sociogram'). That is, the process can move back and forwards between strategic sociometry, classical sociometry, action methods, and encounter.

Strategic methods tend to reveal a circuit of interactions around an identified problem – in this case, a fight. Duane wants to discern and make known to the group the forbidden agendas, the coalition alignments around the problem. He wishes to keep people's relationships as fluid as possible, because after a period of time in a group or organization, choice-making activity becomes patterned. But if the group system of forbidden agendas is revealed or defined, it becomes freer to change. So Duane asks:

Q: Who is most upset by this problem? A: Jane.
Q: What does Jane do when she is upset? A: She cries.
Q: Who sympathizes with her most when she cries? A: Andrew.
Q: Who becomes most guilty when she cries? A: Cindy.
Q: Who becomes stuck when Andrew sympathizes with Jane? A: Lucy.

As a result of these questions, the group coalitions around a problem start to be revealed, not merely to the director, but to the members themselves. These coalitions are the business of the group, around which most of its dynamics run. Duane wants to create the possibility of alternative epistemologies about the group, new ways in which people make meaning. He also seeks an increase in 'membership' in the problem, and greater freshness and spontaneity.

Fighting itself, apparently a spontaneous enough activity, may actually have become part of the group's linear hypothesis, and is therefore a rigid rather than a spontaneous response. Duane's questions accordingly are designed to provoke new possibilities, new thought, new angles, and new emotional states. They invite group cohesion (by crossing over alliances and coalitions), and enhance creativity. That is, the aim of strategic sociometry is similar to the aims of most action work: the development of spontaneity and the creation of new roles. But the whole group moves to these new roles in a co-evolutionary fashion; the old roles become 'impossible' to hold in the group. Duane's intervention is based on three principles: Co-evolution, Responsiveness to Difference, and Shifting the Frame of Thought.

Co-evolution

In any ecology, all elements are in relationship and continually accommodate to each other. A 'group' quickly forms a kind of ecology, and as quickly requires a concept of co-evolution for it to change. Rather than a simple linear notion of 'individual growth', or even one of 'group-minus-leader growth', a total concept of group-and-leader is required. Once the group has formed, the director-and-group attempt to co-evolve. Ecologically speaking, if any one member changes, the others must adjust. Duane's questions are therefore formulated in the light of hypotheses about holistic patterns within the system.

He is attempting to illustrate a notion of reciprocity among the members. He describes the behaviour of one group member and asks another to comment on the reactions of other group members to it. More 'heretically' still, according to some circles of therapy, Duane sometimes even asks person A to assign responsibility to C, D, E, F, or G for person B's behaviour. For example, he once said to Milton, 'You are acting very depressed today' (describes behaviour) and then immediately turned to another member and asked: 'Sally, who in the group is most responsible for keeping Milton depressed?' (assigns responsibility).

After a few answers, the whole group can immediately be invited to go into action on their own behalf in a way whereby Milton's depression is not treated as an isolated or purely personal event: 'Everyone, form a sculpture around Milton to show the ways you keep him depressed.' This could be followed by another instruction: "Now form a sculpture to show how Milton stops you doing anything to change this.'

This procedure is based on a different philosophy from that espoused by many 'fulfilment psychologies', which urge ever more 'responsibility' for the self. Instead, the method advocated here continually places a context around the self of other people's reactions or anticipations – what Moreno calls 'the invisible tele-structures which influence his position' (1953, p. 95). Duane's perceptual test assumes that all roles are interpersonal, consisting not only of cognition, affect, and behaviour, but also of context and effect. What is the effect of Milton's depression? What is the interpersonal context (the group) in which it takes place? Who does Milton hope to influence by his depression?

The assumption that Milton's depression is not merely an 'internal' matter sounds at first risky or even crazy, but if asked, most members will make some sense out of it. The meaning that they assign will usually concern their own lack of spontaneity in their behaviour to Milton. Perhaps they 'walk on egg-shells'; perhaps they also have become depressed; perhaps they become very jolly. Some might see that rather than them containing Milton's depression by their sympathy, he is in fact 'controlling' them, by somehow 'making' them suppress their spontaneous reactions. Or perhaps Milton is trying to help the group in some way by being depressed – a way he may have learned in his family of origin. The questions induce a different way of thinking about events in the group.

Old patterns of thinking and feeling are inevitably revised in a co-evolutionary framework. The context of a member's behaviour is established as paramount, intricately connected with the behaviour of all the other members. So-called 'pathology' becomes seen as a form of social interaction. The person involved and the group itself are defined by the nature of the questions as producing the best solution possible as they see it. So Milton might see the solution to his problems as 'Be depressed', and the group might see the solution to the problem that Milton's depression poses for them as 'Walk on egg-shells'. When these adopted solutions are exposed, other solutions become possible for all.

Co-evolutionary thinking also applies when a person shows heightened spontaneity and flexibility. The social context of our actions is not confined to troubling behaviour. People actually do enhance each other's well-being and help create new and splendid roles. At such times, instead of simply noting the changes to the person involved ('It's great that you're participating more, Mona') the director can congratulate the whole group for the person's new-found freedom, and ask them what they, rather than the individual concerned, did to bring it about:

Tom, who in the group made most space for Mona to participate?
Who is most pleased that she has?
Who do you think will be next to participate more fully?

People thus learn about reciprocity of relationships: 'We have helped M change by changing ourselves as we relate to her.' Praise and blame begin to lose meaning in favour of an understanding that action always takes place in context.

Difference

I have consistently argued in this book that what helps people change is difference that in some way becomes 'news' to them. There are innumerable differences that are not 'news'. Bateson (1982, pp. 108–109) observed that people find it difficult to detect gradual change, because they become habituated and unaware of slow alterations. A person scarcely notices the differences in light through the year as the seasons change; but he or she would notice if it suddenly grew dark at 5 p.m. in the middle of summer. To be perceptible, change must be of sufficient magnitude or sufficient suddenness so that its difference makes an impact. Another reliable way of helping people notice change is to put two things, or two stories, side by side.

Asking a question about the difference in how Cindy and Lucy regard Mollie's behaviour attracts awareness of that difference. If Bateson is right, Cindy can only understand her behaviour in terms of (a) difference from someone else (although the person chosen need not necessarily be Lucy - that will depend on the director's hypothesis), or (b) difference between now and at some time in the past, or between now and some time in the future. For differences to become 'information' they must be differences that make a difference – they must be relevant. I am different from a tennis racquet, but that difference is not usually a relevant one.

One of the shapes that 'difference' questions can take is the before/after form. That is, the comparisons can relate to changes in the mood state of the group or changes in 'hidden sociometry' after a particular event. For example, supposing the group seems tense and 'flighty', but Duane does not know what has triggered this state. His strategic sociometry could run something like the following:

D: *When did the problem in the group begin?*
Jill: *Three weeks ago.*
D: *What else was happening three weeks ago?*
Jill: *Sandy didn't turn up for two sessions in a row.*
D: *Who missed her most?*
Jill: *Judith and Bob and Cindy.*
D: *Who had the hardest time adjusting?*
Mike: *Bob.*
D: *Why?*
Mike: *She drives home with him when the group is finished and they talk.*
D: *Who in the group most wished they didn't do that?*
Jill: *You, Duane (laughter) and Carol and Cindy.*
D: *Andrew, do you agree with Jill that me and Carol and Cindy are most against Sandy and Bob driving home together? etc.*

The event of Sandy missing the group twice running has become tied into a system of relationships that tend to be 'the' secrets of the group. Particular contents of the group secrets are not so much the forbidden agendas as who shares the secrets. Thus Judith, Bob, and Cindy are linked in that they all missed Sandy for various reasons. In the example, these reasons were not explored, but they could have been. Bob and Sandy have a 'driving home' alliance, where presumably many opinions are shared. The people who are thought most to object to this alliance (including the director) are identified, and the reasons why they object could also be developed.

Alternatively, a new set of alliances over the same issue can be explored from a different angle. For example: 'Who doesn't give a damn that Bob drives home with Sandy? . . . How do you explain that M doesn't give a damn?' The 'why' questions are not so much designed to diagnose people's motivations, as to uncover the unexpressed values of the group on the issue (the group myth). The myth might be that the group will come to some harm if Bob and Sandy drive home together. It is then important to search out the alliances around this belief – who believes it, who does not. Who agrees with whom?

A group can be asked to shape their comments to each other in terms of differences, rather than absolute judgements. The information relevant to people in a group is usually called 'feedback'. Feedback that is given early on in a group is generally of the order 'You are X' or 'You are Y' – for example, 'You are defensive, Mark' or 'You are completely cut off from your feelings, Moira'. That is, the giver of the feedback makes an assumption that he or she is an objective judge of the other person's behaviour. This form of feedback is not highly regarded in therapeutic circles, although, for some clients or patients, the ability to make any direct statement to another person may quite rightly be considered as a step in the right direction.

Later, after careful tutelage from the leader, the nature of the feedback is likely to change. The feedback 'I see you doing such and such' is linked with self-disclosure, 'This is how I experience myself'. Members begin to express themselves in 'I statements' that are incorporated into the 'you' statements of feedback. That is, comments are couched in terms of their reaction to the other person: 'When you are silent, Mick, I feel like I'm hammering on a locked door', or 'When I talk to you, Moira, I can feel the life draining away from me'. This type of comment blending feedback and self-disclosure is expressed in terms of a relationship. Such commentary is more recursive than simple feedback or simple self-disclosure, and is usually regarded as beneficial for the giver and receiver alike.

I have argued throughout this book, and in *The Passionate Technique*, for relationship or 'difference' as the form by which people know things. Strategic sociometry extends but by no means replaces relationship-style feedback. In the first example of this chapter, where Mollie was fighting with Maria, the relationship between Cindy and Lucy is gathered together around the event, and their reactions are compared in terms of one or other being 'more upset' when Mollie gets angry. The comment, by Bob, produces complex feedback to Cindy, to Lucy, to Mollie, and to Maria on their impact on the system, and the system's impact on them. Moreover, as the comment is made in comparative terms, it is presumably more intelligible than some sort of absolute judgement (e.g. 'You are shy' or 'You are suspicious'), where the receiver is left with a problem of meaning: Just how shy, how suspicious is one? What does it mean? Compare these statements with 'You are shyer/more suspicious than you used to be' or '. . . than Cindy is'. These concepts are more manageable than when expressed in absolute terms. The comparisons, with before/after or with Cindy, are not meant to engender competition, but merely to create meaning.

Shifting the frame of thought

When strategic directors fashion a criterion, they tend positively to connote the contexts of events. Positive connotation brings new information to the group by shifts in the framework of the leader's and the members' thinking (the belief aspects of their roles). Sociometric criteria do not merely elicit information about groupings around a certain point; they also introduce concepts, as we have seen. Take the question: 'Who would be the first to recognize that Mollie gets angry because she cares too much rather than too little?' The new concept in that example is 'caring too much'.

A strategic criterion might, for instance, embed the notion of volition as against things just happening: 'When Mollie decided to get angry. . . .', 'When did Milton make up his mind to be depressed?' Other concepts such as 'caring for others when they are distressed', or 'curiosity', or 'courage' can be introduced by questions such as 'Who in the group is most curious about what will happen next?', thus providing a helpful connotation for otherwise negative and pathologizing labels such as 'symbiotic depression', 'anticipitatory anxiety', and the like. Criteria can also be selected on the grounds of people's grouping around an event and not merely an emotional state. For example, Sandy's absence can be reconstrued as 'leaving the group on the shelf', so that the group's former anger at the 'abandonment' element of the absence can take on a new light.

The frame-shift acts as a brake on linear thinking and advice. Sometimes linear feedback ('You are X; you are Y') becomes a problem-maintaining rather than problem-solving device. For example, Mollie might traditionally receive 'feedback' (covert advice) on whether she ought to be 'more' or 'less' angry. Now it may well be that she has already given herself plenty of 'feedback' on this matter in her own self-talk, and has perhaps done so for years, without getting very far. But if the question becomes 'Who in the group is most relieved when Mollie gets mad?', the focus is shifted away from whether Mollie should or should not control her temper. The new focus is the function of Mollie's temper in the group. What does it do for Mollie; what does it do for the group? The question of 'relief' puts the outburst into a different frame. Judith can begin to see that her outbursts may be serving 'group needs', such as to be distracted, to be a victim, to be part of an aggressive interaction without seeming to be, or whatever. The questions for her, then, become how much longer will she go on 'serving' the group in this way, and what does being angry in this way do for her?'

The rest of the group also have to deal with the event in ways that they have not formerly considered. The 'feedback' is multiple, as the director drives at a system reaction to the event – how the dyadic behaviour between Mollie and Maria is established and maintained by the group.

In a group, change has the best chance of occurring when the support systems of dysfunctional patterns are challenged and undermined. If the group members are, in fact, 'relieved' by the incident, the chances are that the anger outbursts will happen over and over again, much to Mollie and Maria's bewilderment. It seems as if everyone is 'out of control' – the principal actors, and those who maintain them. Mollie's individual desires to be 'less' angry are not irrelevant, but sociometric criteria revealing 'relief' in the group when she is angry may help her to see what she must confront in trying to be 'less' angry; how the 'we' influences the 'I'.

As for Maria, it would be easy to become unhelpfully caught up in her misery if one looked only at her individual roles. A strategic director, however, is most interested in Maria's group roles. When this set of roles is considered, the question of Maria's 'function' in the system may become more intelligible. If Maria's major group roles were, say, Scapegoat and Victim, one of the important figures nominated as 'most relieved when Mollie gets angry' might be Maria herself. As a result of the information, Maria may recognize and wish to change her group function of Scapegoat and Victim.

Applications

Restraints can operate at an individual or group level, causing people to see only one possible way of acting. Whether the problem concerns within- or extra-group functioning, the outsider becomes a blinker-remover, easing the restraints so that people within the group can find new ways of looking at things. Members are enlarged by the world-view of the others in the group. As the restraints on holding only one story lift, members become more spontaneous, more capable of new ways of thinking, feeling, and acting. Spontaneity is nothing less than a capacity for adaptive functioning; it is not whimsy or fecklessness, even when sometimes the ways of accessing it are deliberately eccentric. Life itself sets the boundaries, and though, as Eric Bentley (1972) remarked, action methods move the boundary posts a little, they do not throw them away.

Since its chief focus is on alliances, triangles, and sub-groupings, strategic sociometry is most appropriately used in an established group or organization. It is not a way of running a group as such, but is intended as an occasional 'unlocking' device for a system that has become stuck. Revealing the forbidden agendas in the group tends to shift stuck habits of thinking. This occasionally-to-be-used way of intervening leads the group to a very 'quiet' form of spontaneity. After a run of strategic questions, members tend to be calm, and ready to get on with whatever the group has gathered together to do. The 'spontaneity' involved seems to be a new way of thinking which clears the way for new emotional interactions. It is a 'cool' rather than a 'hot' medium, even though the issue involved – alliances, including alliances with the leader – is the 'hottest' topic a group can touch (Yalom, 1975).

In the author's experience, the method appears to do one thing well: it provides multiple perspectives that clear the group for work. The group seems no longer to operate as a 'basic assumption' group, but as a 'work' group (Bion, 1961). That is, members can do what they came to do. After a successful 'run' of strategic questions, the passions tied up by the forbidden agendas are cooler, for a while anyway.

Chapter fourteen

Conclusion – a living aesthetic

Language is like a cracked kettle on which we beat out tunes for bears to dance to, while all the time we long to move the stars to pity.

Gustave Flaubert

Alas for all that expensive psychological training! As often as not, the 'high points' of an action group come not from directors' deep therapeutic insights, but from their abilities as producers. This may sound a little shocking, when one thinks of what a 'psychological', complicated, and high-minded endeavour consultancy is. How alarming if success as an action methods director were to boil down to this: how well can you put on a story? Fortunately (because aesthetics are more difficult to understand and teach than pragmatics) it is not quite so. Directors at least need to know their epistemology, if not their psychology (provided those two are different, that is). Nevertheless, it would be hard to overestimate the effect of beauty, economy, form, and power in an action group, and so 'Putting on the story' is the focus of this final chapter.

The aesthetics of action methods are the 'wild card' of change. They compel us finally to go beyond pragmatics to account for someone being different after an action group. If you have been in such a group, you will remember how tension and excitement build up the minute competent directors externalize the protagonist's imagery, turning linguistic clues into dramatic action. If they make the production line the same as the lifeline of the subject, the audience too stays engaged. The relentless tug of the narrative pulls along everyone with it.

The routine is by now familiar to you: as rapidly as possible, directors gain a sense of the issues and possible directions that the drama might take – otherwise they will get mixed up in messy role reversals and unaesthetic clutter. Director and protagonist 'co-visualize' a scene as it is taking shape. They are alive to the formal qualities of the action as much as their therapeutic import. They ask questions such as 'Is anything missing?', or 'What colour is the bench top?' These apparently trivial strokes often provide a key to the entire staging of the drama, and help protagonists warm up to a scene that otherwise could have been flat and lifeless. I recall directing a drama with a young woman who had been sexually abused as a girl: the entire success of the drama depended on her remembering the pattern of the linoleum floorcovering in her childhood bedroom, and the shape of the cupboard in the corner. (As it turned out, the cupboard was backless and gave way to a disused staircase of the public building which the father owned, and from which he would make good his escape.)

That is an example of success from a drama chiefly being due to elaborate scene-setting. (The drama eventually turned into a violent confrontation between the protagonist and her father, by the way, and led to lasting changes in the protagonist's life – scholastically, socially, and even physically.) At other times 'less is more', as the saying goes, and economy is the key, as in the example of 'The Bird of Death', below. Simplicity is hard-won, too.

The bird of death

Maggie is visibly upset in the group after a bird has crashed into the window and died. The whole group was also shocked by this event, but had moved on. Two hours later, Delia, the director, notices that Maggie still looks dazed and abstracted. She asks her if she wants to do anything about being upset. Maggie hesitates, and then nods 'yes'.

Delia creates an instant 'stage', moving the group out of its circle shape and into a horseshoe, preparatory to a drama. She calls on two of the group members at random to stand on the stage and to act as if they were holding a sheet of glass between them. She says to Maggie 'Be a bird'.

In a strategic interview, as we shall see, the director inquires as to the complaint, what the previous solutions have been, and what would be an acceptable outcome if the drama were successful. After even the most 'pragmatic' drama starts, however, neither actor nor director are able to work with complete intentionality. They are involved in making up a new reality, designed during the process, which exploits the dramatic capacities of the scene. They embrace the comic, the violent, or the simply wacky, trusting that the integrity of this method will bring them to a new truth.

Once a drama begins, irrational and spontaneous factors enter stage left, and the pragmatic has to hang on tight to keep its place in the cast. The pragmatics of change now rely on an overall strategic frame for the consultancy set up at the beginning, rather than what will happen moment to moment. What happens moment to moment is in the lap of the imagination.

Maggie bird-like spreads her arms and begins to move. She swoops around the room, perching briefly on a chair, and then taking off again. She glides, or flaps vigorously. Though she never seems to pay any attention to the glass, the dialogue is already there. It is made necessary, just by the two of their presences: bird and glass.

This is obviously a dance, an enactment of a dialectic between life and death. The audience tenses as it watches this simple and most wordless of dramas. Suddenly, BANG! she hits the glass, and falls down immediately. She is perfectly still for a minute, and then begins to weep jarringly and gracelessly. She is raw, true, and oblivious to everything except her dialogue with death.

Her cries eventually purge her heart of its grief. When she dries up, which she does after a little while, she says that she would like Georgie, the youngest member of the group, to be the bird. The 'window' is taken away, and Georgie flies around solo, while Maggie sits on the floor and watches her. This lasts for about two minutes. Maggie says to her: 'I can't protect you . . . ultimately I can't do it. For now I can keep some of the gross dangers away, but in the end you're on your own, kid.'

Why did this drama work, because 'work' it did? At follow-up several months later, Maggie still remembered it with affection, even though the experience had initially been a harrowing one. She reported that she felt more accepting and less anxious. . . .

I was able to look at something, my fears about my own death, and having to leave my eight-year-old son behind. But I saw the dance could continue without me – I could sit down and watch him keep dancing. Before, I'd thought about living and dying only intellectually. But in the drama I could really experience the feeling. I could project my death into the future and really feel it.

The effects from her involvement were quite profound, not only in relation to her and her child, but in terms of taking responsibility

for other things in my life while I am here. . . . It gave me permission to be more here and now, and not so worried about the future. . . . I'm saying yes to a lot more things and taking on more. For a long time I'd had a great sense of powerlessness, and I was angry at that. I felt minute and not able to make a difference to anything. That's not so now.

Maggie's drama is a little inconveniently successful, because more complexity must now be included in the explanation than you have been given so far. You see, unfortunately for the neatness of this text, but true to the complexity of life, Delia has wandered through several of the boundaries that I have so far been at pains to wire up. Action methods can be as intense and unforgettable as any experience that we think of as 'real'. They can also be trash, full of strident heroics and naive romanticism. But when people act, move, or talk in ways that are right for them, as Miller (1980, p. 89) remarks, their activities exhibit 'those qualities by which we judge art – economy and gracefulness, necessity and flexibility'. Whether the process is trash or treasure depends on the aesthetics, and on whether it leads to genuinely new avenues of being.

One reason for the success of the 'Bird of Death' vignette may have been that Delia operated primarily as an artist. Working aesthetically does not mean making things pretty. A drama looks good when it enfleshes an ultimate unity: aesthetic affirmation comes when somehow we are able to glimpse that whatever the ups and downs of detail, the larger whole is primarily beautiful (Bateson, 1979, p. 27). In dialectic with the larger whole is the fragility of beings-in-time. This, perhaps, is what makes great works of art great. Aesthetic preferences are expressed through intuition, love, playfulness, and a kind of poetic logic. These modes of relating, says Allman (1982), sometimes transcend deductive logic and dispense with illusions of total control over nature. By relating aesthetically to others and the environment, people participate in the wholeness of their lived experience. Since that is one of the aims of consultation anyway, maybe there is not so much conflict between aesthetics and pragmatics as may first appear.

So while this book has been much concerned with the pragmatics of consultation, it may now be understood that the aesthetic and the pragmatic do not have to negate each other. Indeed, the pragmatic emerges out of the aesthetic as simply one of a multitude of possible ways of construing events: access to action and beauty can lead to the realization of new and creative solutions to old problems quite as well as the tightest of behavioural programmes. Good works of art seem to contain an inexhaustible supply of new information: 'We can return again and again to a masterpiece and come away refreshed. This is what Ezra Pound meant when he said "Poetry is news that stays news". How it manages to do so remains mostly mysterious' (Miller, 1980, p. 88).

Maybe Maggie did not need any more than what she got, and Delia did not need to do any more than she did. It was enough for Maggie to 'externalize' her story and see it in front of her. Through having to be an actor, she was continually brought to the point of spontaneity, the moment of creation itself. In fact, she not only created on stage her 'first story' as the bird destined for its tragic end; she also created a second story that was not so oppressive, when she asked Georgie, the auxiliary, to dance for her. She attained a 'double description' between the first and second story. Her drama was characterized by a spare aesthetic which led her to spontaneity; she thought new thoughts, and, though it may not have done so without Delia's responding to responses, the new description of herself outlasted the old.

The cross-country skier

Even though action methods involve rough drama, unrehearsed drama, they still need a shape. It only seems as if the protagonist attends to the narrative and the form arrives completely simultaneously and 'out of the blue'. That this sometimes does happen is often an illusion created by the co-operation of a skilled director with a kind of 'will' that the dramatic process itself has towards form. The authenticity of the human experience being re-created gives the action a kind of teleology towards beauty, softness, and strength – we are back to the chrysanthemum of the Introduction. Authentic dramas tend to look good: somehow the exact symbol is presented – a bird, a brooch, a phrase from childhood. This image concentrates and purifies the meaning emerging in the narrative. Directors need at least enough 'feel' to intuit which one to select, and enough grace not to put their own sentimentality or therapeutic preconceptions in the way when something authentic, severe, or beautiful is happening. All going well, the new form that director and protagonist co-create becomes saturated with possibilities, providing occasion for play and discovery of a second description.

Melissa still feels the loss of her father, who died two years previously. She frequently cries in the group, and cannot concentrate on what is going on, no matter how hard she tries. Although she is continually upset, days pass before she feels ready to offer herself for a drama. On the last day before the consultant is due to leave the group, she says that she is ready, and that the matter is quite urgent.

Duane asks her to describe what sort of man her father was. It seems that he was an admirable person – a retired schoolteacher who had been very fond of sport. In his younger days he had been an excellent sailor, cricketer, and footballer. About two years before his death he had taken up cross-country skiing. He was also very keen on wild country, and would love to go bushwalking. In fact, he had set up a native garden in the front of his house, while Melissa's mother had a more exotic garden in the back.

At the time of his final illness, the father had become very agitated. Melissa, then in her mid-thirties, was called to the house to restrain him as he kept trying to go out the front door. (The first scene of the drama takes place in the hallway, where Father, near death, is crying wildly: 'Outside. Outside. Outside.') In reality, the family did restrain him, and forcibly led him back to bed where he was given a sedative. The next day he died. Melissa had never forgiven herself for what she saw as her harsh and controlling actions in his last hours.

A drama is enacted of these moments. First 'how it was' (that is, Melissa's story of the events); and then re-enacted in surplus reality. Duane asks Melissa to reverse roles as the father. In the interview, the father says that he just wants to go out into his garden, which reminds him of his beloved wild country. He does this, and is very happy. After relaxing in his garden, inspecting some of his favourite trees and rocks, he says that it is now time for him to go. Duane suggests that since it is snowing, he may need his skis. The father agrees, and skis off after the tenderest farewells with his family.

Melissa (back as herself) asks him whether he minded the incident of being forced back to bed and being given drugs. As the father, in role reversal, he laughs, and says that it was the tiniest hiccup in a long and very happy life. He pats Melissa on the head reassuringly, but without sentimentality, and then skis away, getting smaller and smaller – he progressively bobs down to give the effect – through the 'trees' (also played by members of the group, who are all crying, as is Duane himself).

Only rarely is one's brief simply to put on something that is beautiful or elevated. Only rarely is the consultant engaged as an artist/theologian, charged with directing transformational events to give culture and persons back to themselves. Be that as it may, it would appear that even the most 'pragmatic' work in action seems 'accidentally' to leave little clues lying around concerning the numinous; they are like straying spouses, at some level wanting to be found out, leaving double theatre tickets sticking out of their shirt pockets after 'working late at the office'.

A few weeks after this elegiac drama, Melissa reported the following to Duane and the group: 'After we left, I felt wonderful. It gave me the good things. I found my father again. Also I felt I lost him. Since he died, I had felt too close to him in my mind; now I feel he's gone. I felt down at some level, but much more whole. I talked to my mum about his death, and cried in front of her – that's most unusual. I was glad to do that. It made me feel better about another crazy incident that happened about three years ago that I don't want to go into now. I seemed to others to be going mad. It now feels like a big shift that will come out gradually. I can just start talking to people, not knowing what I am going to say. I initiate relationships more. I'm much more assertive.'

Melissa, like Maggie, certainly reported many effects of the drama that could not have been predicted by what actually happened in it. The session's power partly came from its aesthetics of form and mood –

Duane's picking up the father's love of sport, the significance of the front garden, and weaving these into a metaphor for departure. Melissa and Duane co-created a piece that had a strong aesthetic resonance for her and the group. The father's skiing off provided an ending that was uniquely and properly dramatic; it could not have come about had only 'psychological' rather than formal qualities of her discourse been taken into account. A conversational or 'therapeutic' resolution to the loss would have been quite different from a dramatic resolution.

A dramatic resolution does not simply mean the discharge of raw emotion. Simple discharge of emotion is neither good art nor good therapy. Only a very romanticized Freudianism or Morenianism would assume that when the unconscious opens, out pours Art. Memories, emotions, and dreams may well tap the sources of spontaneity, but in themselves they are incomplete and unformed. Though it may not appear so to the unaccustomed eye, a successful drama is not just 'experience', but experience reorganized, edited, and choreographed.

Timing and contrast

The formal qualities of action methods demand a keen sense of timing, not only for role reversals, but for the introduction and re-introduction of key figures. Elements of the drama are selected, condensed, repeated, and formalized. This is why it is sometimes helpful to hold protagonists back from premature enactment, by insisting on certain details, or maintaining the drama at interview stage a little longer, or by delaying the entry of certain key figures until the precisely appropriate moment. When this moment comes, it is as though a tripwire has been touched, springing the drama open. Unexpectedly, we all fall through its trapdoor.

Restraining the action until it is time, until the protagonist is properly warmed up, pays off in sequences that are more economical and elegant. Gross urging from the director to maximize and repeat actions, typical of coarse psychodrama, become unnecessary. This sort of hectoring and badgering would be unacceptable in a theatre, and can well be avoided in an action group, too. What is required is to get right the dynamics of staging and the articulation of relationships. Consider this unpromisingly abstract start:

M: *Inside my head, things are going whiz, whiz, whiz.*
D: *How many things are there?*
M: *(surprised) Uh, three, I think.*
D: *Choose three people from the group to be those things.*
(M does so)
Reverse roles with one of them.
(M does so)

Good evening. Who are you?
V1: *I hate him. I tell him he's bad.*
D: *Do you now? Show us what you do.*
(The first voice begins to weave in and out, making little darting motions at M)
D: *(To auxiliary, now V1): Keep doing that.*
(To M): Reverse roles with another of the voices.

The director continues in this vein until all the voices and their movements have been set up. She then gets the voices to interact with each other. Only when all this is done does she ask M to resume his own role and respond. The tension involved in holding M back until the whole system is set up actually triggers the drama (which is not reported here).

It would be quite silly to pretend that the above is great art or even great therapy. The director did her best to transform M's experience so that he could develop a new integration. She takes what is structureless, and works with M to give it form.

Acting is a way of knowing that involves feeling, impression, and imagination. As well as using words to create a description or definition, actors use form, even though that form be as embryonic as the 'things' in the example above. The form is simultaneously discovered and created by a sort of instinct that is more direct than the instinct governing speech. Decisions are made by a sixth sense. In making up one's life, things happen so fast: one moves to the centre of one's being, as it were. Once there, the tension of being held back, if only for a moment, deepens the warm-up. By being caught in the act, the feeling is of acute surrender wherein lies power. Directors may have to blunder along through early material in a drama until they can find a suitable level of aesthetic co-creation with the protagonist. The drama relies as much on the aesthetic sense of the protagonist as it does with that of the director.

Action can express our inner modes of being, and give tangible form to psychological states. These 'psychological states', however, are usually plaited in with other people's stories, as I have already remarked. We are never quite alone: the other person is always there, vital as the object of speech or love. The dramatic process presents to others our correlates for feeling and interaction; both our inner states and our 'between-ness' are put concretely 'out there', as form. Yet the final form, the result of the action, is not known at the time.

Members usually work from prior experience. They start with the first story which they have always seen as 'the truth'. In the process of setting out their first story, probably for the first time, new experience occurs. There is little need to create the second story – it creates itself, as often as not, merely by full enactment of the first. The group member in the instance reported below tries to warm himself up by shouting. Instead of instantly 'maximizing' the loud emotion of M's 'inside wanting to burst out', the director works by contrast, giving the piece more rhythmic buoyancy. Though this is no Shakespeare or Chekhov at work, the forms created will probably do the job well enough.

M: *(Defiantly) I've got a feeling of being angry with the whole of life. In my mother's case she died in the course of events. She manifested 'yes' to life. She went on. The experience of people who need and want to die angers me. It wasn't meant to be that way.*

D: *(Temporarily ignoring the cue about mother's death) Show us the bits you're feeling angry with.*

M: *(Chooses three people who link hands) I don't know if it's my inside wanting to burst out, or the whole of life. . . . It's like things out there, and they're inside me as well. (Cries out) Why do people want to die! (Shouts melodramatically) Why do people want to die!*

D: *Reverse roles with one of these other people.*

M: *(As containing triangle) I don't hear you.*

D: *Reverse roles, and be yourself.*

M: *(As himself, very still now) That's what it's like. Nobody hears.*

D: *Use the whole stage. Get tables and chairs, and stand as high as you can. Now, shout 'Why do people want to die?' Then, as far away as you need, and being as small as you need, place another part of you that whispers 'Nobody hears'. Whisper it as softly as you can.*

M: *(Does all this)*
Good, now choose from the group someone who can be your mum, and have a talk with her.

Action can throw rope bridges across categories formerly cut by chasms, and even though one might sway on them a bit, find that experience is not so fragmented after all. It is possible to take a wobbly walk across, as M did in the vignette above. The swaying ropes are only anchored at either side by intuition and felt meaning. It may seem strange to refer to these as 'anchors', since we are accustomed to regarding them as the most ephemeral of all our processes. At least in human affairs, though, access to intuition and felt meaning (Bateson, 1979) is just about the only thing we can rely on.

A different form of logic from conversational logic prevails, and different thinking pathways are involved which in themselves can lead to spontaneity, new possibility. The requirements of action imply that the protagonist has to enter a new set of relationships with the people depicted in the drama. Though some of the process may be irrational and odd, the aim is not so much a crude expression of feeling, as to define members' lives according to all the relevant connections. These definitions of their lives, their maps of reality, take the form of narrative and description. The descriptions, the definitions, are done in visual and kinaesthetic terms so that not so much a logical as a sensory intelligence comes into play.

Indeed, 'play' can be one of the main operators, since by play one comes across the unexpected, and the unexpected demands new roles – spontaneity. In the following extract, the director herself needs to do very little except to stay out of the way and to give a nudge or two at the appropriate time. The group warms itself up to a new direction by playing with imagery and giving it physical expression.

M1: *I want to move on. I feel we're bogged.*
M2: *(Ecstatic at the prospect of action after an hour or so of dull talk) Maybe we can do a vision of a bog. Let's have quicksand, let's have straggling vines, let's do the work.*
M3: *(Joins her, playschool-like) I'd be into that. Us being sucked down.*
M2: *Let's have it over here in this part of the room.*
M1: *A vehicle stuck in lots of oozy mud.*
(Goes on hands and knees and thrashes behind) There's lots of mud oozing behind.
D: *What else can you see, hear, or smell?*
M1: *I can smell the fumes from the engine.*
D: *Anything else that's important?*
M1: *No.*
D: *Reverse roles with the mud.*
M1: *(Sonorously) I am the power of the mud. You can't escape from the power of the mud. (Crawls all over the vehicle) It slowly goes down and I cover it (laughs maniacally). They all stay stuffed there. They have to die!*
D: *Reverse roles and be the engine.*
M1: *(As engine) I get out.*
(She immerses herself in the mud as an engine,and struggles under several group members to get out. When she does manage, the group cheers. They all resume places in the circle.)

Well . . . has anything been achieved? Should M1's 'anal fixation' and 'sadism' ('. . . lots of mud oozing behind' and 'They have to die. . .') have been elaborated and interpreted? Has the group 'got' anywhere by this sort of horsing around? In terms of 'therapy', maybe not. But perhaps one need not get too sententious about everything that happens in a group, and elevate it either to high drama or an important cure for souls. A little 'horsing around' can develop imagination and contribute to the group's ability to deal in fresh ways with problems. Dramatic play is not the *raison d'être* of a problem-focused group, but nor is it out of place. It builds resources in the group for action, for liveliness, and for a new kind of problem-solving. Even horsing around can be shapely and satisfying, necessitating a shift to more exciting visual and kinaesthetic patterns. Members' judgements become more aesthetic, involving selection and rejection of material formerly considered not worthy of story.

Action incarnates all the factors in a system so that they become a living presence. An action group gives one a deep feeling for 'what is-ness', and for possibility. It lays these two side by side, creating a double description between the story now and another story. One description lies inside the system's constructs, and the other lies outside, forming a contrast which enhances the system's capacity to receive new ideas. The problem, which has so far seemed integral to reality, is juxtaposed with a different type of reality. The gate to the forbidden city opens a crack, and you are allowed to look in.

I have been arguing through most of this book for adopting certain procedures in action groups with a problem focus. It may well be asked how a minimalist 'strategic' philosophy and practice can fit with that most flamboyant of methods, psychodrama? Surely there is nothing more grand, elaborate, noisy, and full of hope than a psychodrama under full sail. And surely there is nothing so spare, restrained, and pragmatic as the strategic approach? A student once asked: 'If I want to work strategically, do I have to give up the good bits?' I have tried to answer this question at length in *The Passionate Technique*, where I distinguished psychodrama as Revelation from psychodrama as Therapy. The short answer is 'no' – nothing need be lost except muddle. No beauty, no glory, no majesty need be abandoned. On the other hand, when one is working for change, Beauty, Glory, and Majesty do have to go into harness and pull a cart or two – they cannot merely stand in a field and chew.

Where 'revelation' or 'epiphany' is agreed as the rationale, the charter is more open for transformational drama. Beauty, Glory, and Majesty can stand in a field without their harnesses, and be admired for their looks. Notions of 'problem', 'customer', and 'complaint' can be forgotten, and the director can let the drama go with nothing more in mind than rich experiences. Even here, a drama needs a structure, otherwise it would not even be a rich experience, but airy, tawdry, and pretentious. Airy, Tawdry, and Pretentious are no good at pulling carts, and do not even look good when they are standing and chewing.

Just as an admirable building, painting, novel, or poem has a structure which is as tough as nails, so an action format needs to be structurally sound ('Finding a voice'). I have been suggesting that it is sound practice to ask that a problem about which there is a 'complaint' ('Warm-up to what?') be put in solvable form so that the complainant becomes a 'customer' for change ('Focusing the conflict'). Working strategically does not mean playing hard-ball or ugly-ball. Competent directors recognize that people sometimes find it difficult to formulate how they want things to be different – if they could do it easily, they may not have summoned a consultant in the first place. They help clients with this task, assuming good faith ('Ideas for an outsider'), and knowing from their own lives what human frailty is.

But it is not 'more humanistic' to be confused about one's working arrangements, or to assume one knows what people want when in fact one may not know. Nor is it an anti-dramatic act of meanness to follow up a piece of action, asking about changes week by week ('Responding to responses'). On the contrary, it seems a kindness to assume that one's work will 'work', and that there will be a time, often a short one, when group members will go home and stay there. Ultimately, the task is to make 'home' a better place to go to, rather than the group the best place to stay in.

This task is easier in individual therapy: a successful action methods group often does seem the best and most exciting place to be, because of the natural aesthetic of drama, and the powerful pull of the group process. Life in the social atom is often not as exciting or as close as it is in the group. The group itself becomes a major part of members' social atom – that is the ethical and therapeutic trap of most groups, and can lead in some cases to consultancy becoming a problem rather than a solution. This two-way stretch of warming up a group enough for cohesion and creativity, at the same time as providing a frame whereby members (and directors) do not forget what they came for has been alluded to constantly.

Firm boundaries and a problem focus, however, do not necessarily mean that one has to give up 'the good bits'. When called for, strategic action methods, too, can be lush and sensual, can co-create worlds of pain, glory, horror, or hilarity as well as any other. Strategic directors well know, like ordinary human beings, the richness of ordinary life and the shaping and sustaining force of love. They also know that problems are often a by-product of this force. Anyone who has seen an action group successfully at work, where the levels of human experience are revealed like geological layers, cannot doubt that at the fossil level, at the level of sedimentary rock, are found the outlines of love, perfectly preserved like ferns – or ancient fish.

References

Agazarian, Y. (1982). Role as a bridge construct in understanding the relationship between the individual and the group. In M. Pines and L. Rafaelson (eds) *The individual and the group, Vol. 1*. New York: Plenum Press.

Agazarian, Y. and Peters, R. (1981). *The visible and invisible group*. London: Routledge & Kegan Paul.

Allman, L. (1982). The aesthetic preference: overcoming the pragmatic error. *Family Process*, *21*, 43–56.

Anderson, H. and Goolishian, H. (1988). Human systems as linguistic systems: preliminary and evolving ideas about the implications of clinical theory. *Family Process*, *27*, 371–393.

Arcaya, J. (1985). Metaphorical analysis and hermeneutical interpretation in analytical group psychotherapy. *Group*, *9*, 17–28.

Bach, G. R. (1954). *Intensive group psychotherapy*. New York: Ronald Press.

Bateson, G. (1958). *Naven*. Stanford: Stanford University Press, second edition.

Bateson, G. (1972). *Steps to an ecology of mind*. New York: Ballantine Books.

Bateson, G. (1979). *Mind and nature: A necessary unity*. New York: Bantam Books.

Bateson, G. (1982). Beyond homeostasis: toward a concept of coherence. *Family Process*, *21*, 21–41.

Bentley, E. (1972). Theatre and therapy. In *Theatre of war*. London: Methuen.

Billow, P. (1977). Metaphor: a review of the psychological literature. *Psychological Bulletin*, *84*, 81–92.

Bion, W. R. (1961). *Experiences in groups*. London: Tavistock.

Blatner, A. (1985). The dynamics of catharsis. *Journal of Group Psychotherapy, Psychodrama and Sociometry*, *37*, 157–166.

Blatner, H. (1989). *Acting-in: Practical applications of psychodramatic methods*. New York: Springer.

Bopp, M. J. and Weeks, G. R. (1983). Dialectical metatheory in family therapy. *Family Process*, *23*, 49–61.

Boszormenyi-Nagy, I. and Spark, G. (1973). *Invisible loyalties: reciprocity in intergenerational family therapy*, New York: Harper & Row.

Braaten, L. J. (1974). Development phases of encounter groups and related intensive groups. *Interpersonal Development*, *5*, 112–129.

Brennan, J. and Williams, A. (1988). Clint and the black sheep. *Journal of Strategic and Systemic Therapies*, *7*, 15–24.

Buchanan, D. (1980). The central concern model: a framework for structuring psychodramatic production. *Journal of Group Psychotherapy, Psychodrama and Sociometry*, *33*, 47–62.
Butler, T. and Fuhriman, A. (1983). Curative factors in group psychotherapy: a review of recent literature. *Small Group Behavior*, *14*, 131–142.
Campernolle, T. (1981). J. L. Moreno: an unrecognized pioneer of family therapy. *Family Process*, *20*, 331–335.
Cecchin, G. (1987). Hypothesizing, neutrality and circulating revisited. *Family Process*, *26*, 405–414.
Clayton, L. (1982). The use of the cultural atom to record personality change in individual psychotherapy. *Journal of Group Psychotherapy, Psychodrama and Sociometry*, *35*, 111–117.
Colliver, R. (1987). Developing teachers' skills in observing and thinking about their teaching practice. Unpublished paper, Perth.
Dalmeau, T. and Dick, B. (1989). *From profane to the sacred: small groups as vehicles for cultural change*. Brisbane, Australia: Interchange.
de Shazer, S. (1982). *Patterns of brief family therapy*. New York: Guilford.
de Shazer, S. (1988). *Clues: investigating solutions in brief therapy*. New York: W. W. Norton.
Dick, B. (1984). *Helping groups to be effective*. Chapel Hill, Queensland: Interchange.
Fisch, R., Weakland, J., and Segal, L. (1982). *The tactics of change: doing therapy briefly*. San Francisco: Jossey Bass.
Fox, J. (1987). *The essential Moreno*. New York: Springer.
French, T. (1952). The integration of behaviour: basic postulates. Chicago: University of Chicago Press.
French, T. (1954). *The integration of behaviour: the integrative process in dreams*. Chicago: University of Chicago Press.
Ginn, R. (1974). Psychodrama, a theatre for our time. *Group Psychotherapy and Psychodrama*, *32*, 123–146.
Goldman, E. and Morrison, D. (1984). *Psychodrama: experience and process*. Dubuque, Iowa: Kendall/Hunt.
Gordon, D. (1978). *Therapeutic metaphors*. Cupertino, Calif.: Meta Publications.
Greenberg, L. (1980). The intensive analysis of recurring events from the practice of Gestalt therapy. *Psychotherapy: Theory, Research and Practice*, *17*, 143–152.
Greenberg, L. (1983). Toward a task analysis in conflict resolution in Gestalt therapy. *Psychotherapy: Theory, Research and Practice*, *20*, 190–201.
Hale, A. (1974). Warm up to a sociometric exploration. *Group Psychotherapy and Psychodrama*, *32*, 1.
Hale, A. E. (1981). *Conducting clinical sociometric exploration: a manual for psychodramatists and sociometrists*. Available from author: 1601 Memorial Avenue, No. 4, Roanoke, VA, 24015, USA.
Hare, A. P. (1986). Moreno's contribution to social psychology. *Journal of Group Psychotherapy, Psychodrama and Sociometry*, *39*, 85–94.
Hart, J. W. and Nath, R. (1979). Sociometry in business and industry: new developments in historical perspective. *Journal of Group Psychotherapy, Psychodrama and Sociometry*, *32*, 128–149.
Heaney, S. (1980). *Preoccupations: Selected Prose 1968–1978*. London: Faber.
Johnstone, K. (1979). *Impro: improvisation and the theatre*. London: Faber.
Keeney, B. P. (1983). *Aesthetics of change*. New York: Guilford.

Keeney, B. P. and Ross, J. M. (1985). *Mind in therapy: constructing family therapies*. New York: Basic Books.
Kelly, G. R. (1955). *The psychology of personal constructs, Vol. 1*. New York: W. W. Norton.
Kibel, H. and Stein, A. (1981). The group-as-a-whole approach: an appraisal. *International Journal of Group Psychotherapy*, *31*, 409–427.
Kobak, R. R. and Waters, D. B. (1984). Family therapy as a rite of passage: play's the thing. *Family Process*, *23*, 89–100.
Kraus, C. (1984). Psychodrama for fallen gods: a review of Morenian theology. *Journal of Group Psychotherapy, Psychodrama and Sociometry*, *37*, 47–66.
Lakoff, G. and Johnson, M. (1980). *Metaphors we live by*. Chicago: University of Chicago Press.
Leveton, E. (1977). *Psychodrama for the timid clinician*. New York: Springer.
Lipchik, E. and de Shazer, S. (1986). The purposeful interview. *Journal of Strategic and Systemic Therapies*, *15*, 88–99.
Marineau, R. F. (1989). *Jacob Levy Moreno, 1889–1974*. London: Tavistock/ Routledge.
Maturana, H. and Varela, F. (1980). *Autopoiesis and cognition: the realization of the living*. Dordrecht, Holland: D. Reidl.
Miller, M. (1980). Notes on art and symptoms. *The Gestalt Journal*, *3*, 86–98.
Moreno, J. L. (1946, 1964, 1972). *Psychodrama, Vol. 1*. New York: Beacon House.
Moreno, J. L. (1953). *Who shall survive*? New York: Beacon House.
Moreno, J. L. (1959). *Psychodrama, Vol. II*. New York: Beacon House.
Moreno, J. L. (1969). *Psychodrama, Vol. III*. New York: Beacon House.
Neimeyer, G. J. (1989). Metaphorical construction and family therapy. Unpublished manuscript, University of Florida, Gainsville, Florida.
Neville, B. (1989). *Educating psyche*. Melbourne: Collins/Dove.
Papp, P. (1983). *The process of change*. New York: Guilford.
Parry, A. (1984). Maturanation in Milan: recent developments in systemic therapy. *Journal of Strategic and Systemic Therapies*, *3*, 35–42.
Penn, P. (1982). Circular questioning. *Family Process*, *21*, 265–280.
Rabkin, R. (1977). *Strategic psychotherapy*. New York: Basic Books.
Rosenblatt, D. (1987). What has love got to do with it? *The Gestalt Journal*, *11*, 63–75.
Rychlak, J. (ed.) (1976). *Dialectic: Humanistic rationale for behavior and development*. Basel: Karger.
Sanders, C. (1985). 'Now I see the difference' – the use of visual news of difference in clinical practice. *Australian and New Zealand Journal of Family Therapy*, *6*, 23–29.
Schechner, R. (1988). *Performance theory*. London: Routledge.
Selvini Palazzoli, M., Boscolo, L., Cecchin, G. F., and Prata, G. (1980). Hypothesizing-circularity-neutrality: three guidelines for the conductor of the session. *Family Process*, *19*, 3–12.
Starr, A. (1977). *Psychodrama: rehearsal for living*. Chicago: Nelson Hall.
Steele, R. (1979). Psychoanalysis and hermeneutics. *International Review of Psychoanalysis*, *6*, 389–411.
Strong, S. (1968). Counseling: An interpersonal influence process. *Journal of Counseling Psychology*, *15*, 215–224.
Tomm, K. (1984). One perspective on the Milan systemic approach: Part II, description of session format, interviewing style and interventions. *Journal of Marital and Family Therapy*, *10*.

Tomm, K. (1987). Interventive interviewing: Part II, reflexive questioning as a means to enable self-healing. *Family Process 26*, 167–184.

Tuckman, B. W. (1965). Developmental sequence in small groups. *Psychological Bulletin*, *63*, 324–399.

Turner, V. (1974). *Dramas, fields and metaphors*. Ithaca: Cornell Univeristy Press.

Watzlawick, P., Weakland, J., and Fisch, R. (1974). *Change: The principles of problem formation and problem resolution*. New York: W. W. Norton.

Weakland, J. (1983). 'Family therapy' with individuals. *Journal of Strategic and Systemic Therapies*, *2*, 1–9.

Weakland, J., Fisch, R., Watzlawick, P., and Bodin, A. (1974). Brief therapy: focused problem resolution. *Family Process*, *13*, 41–68.

Weeks, G. (1977). Toward a dialectical approach to intervention. *Human Development*, *20*, 277–292.

Whitaker, D. (1982). A nuclear and focal conflict model for integrating individual and group level phenomena in psychotherapy groups. In M. Pines and L. Rafaelsen (eds) *The individual and the group. Vol. 1*. New York: Plenum Press.

Whitaker, D. (1985). *Using groups to help people*. London: Routledge & Kegan Paul.

Whitaker, D. and Lieberman, M. (1964). *Psychotherapy through the group process*. New York: Atherton.

White, M. (1983). Anorexia nervosa: a transgenerational system perspective. *Family Process*, *22*, 255–273.

White, M. (1986). Negative explanation, restraint and double description: a template for family therapy. *Family Process*, *25*, 169–184.

White, M. (1988). The process of questioning: a therapy of literary merit? *Dulwich Centre Newsletter*, Winter, 8–14. Adelaide: Dulwich Centre Publications.

White, M. (1989). The externalizing of the problem. *Dulwich Centre Newsletter*, Summer 1988/89. Adelaide: Dulwich Centre Publications.

White, M. and Epston, D. (1989). *Literate means to therapeutic ends*. Adelaide: Dulwich Centre Publications.

Wilber, K. (1977). *The spectrum of consciousness*. Wheaton: Theosophical Publishing House.

Williams, A. (1988). The existential difference. *Family Therapy Case Studies*, *3*, 25–34.

Williams, A. (1989a). *The Passionate Technique: Strategic psychodrama with individuals, families, and groups*. London: Tavistock/Routledge.

Williams, A. (1989b). The problem of the referring person in consultancy. *Journal of Strategic and Systemic Therapies*, *8*, 16–21.

Williams, A. and Foster, L. (1979). The rhetoric of humanistic education. *Journal of Educational Thought*, *13*, 37–52.

Yalom, I. (1975). *The theory and practice of group psychotherapy*. New York: Basic Books.

Name index

Subject index